Lecture Notes in Computer Science 10241

Commenced Publication in 1973
Founding and Former Series Editors:
Gerhard Goos, Juris Hartmanis, and Jan van Leeuwen

More information about this series at http://www.springer.com/series/7410

G. Alan Wang · Michael Chau
Hsinchun Chen (Eds.)

Intelligence and Security Informatics

12th Pacific Asia Workshop, PAISI 2017
Jeju Island, South Korea, May 23, 2017
Proceedings

 Springer

Editors
G. Alan Wang
Virginia Tech
Blacksburg, VA
USA

Hsinchun Chen
The University of Arizona
Tucson, AZ
USA

Michael Chau
The University of Hong Kong
Hong Kong
China

ISSN 0302-9743   ISSN 1611-3349   (electronic)
Lecture Notes in Computer Science
ISBN 978-3-319-57462-2   ISBN 978-3-319-57463-9   (eBook)
DOI 10.1007/978-3-319-57463-9

Library of Congress Control Number: 2017937692

LNCS Sublibrary: SL4 – Security and Cryptology

Printed on acid-free paper

This Springer imprint is published by Springer Nature
The registered company is Springer International Publishing AG
The registered company address is: Gewerbestrasse 11, 6330 Cham, Switzerland

Preface

Intelligence and security informatics (ISI) is concerned with the development of advanced information technologies, systems, algorithms, and databases for national, international, and societal security-related applications, through an integrated technological, organizational, and policy-based approach. In the past decade, the ISI community has experienced tremendous growth and contributed new theories, algorithms, and methods to the understanding, monitoring, and prevention of intelligence- and security-related issues.

The Pacific Asia Workshop on Intelligence and Security Informatics (PAISI) provides a platform for the ISI community to present and discuss findings in security-related research. PAISI 2017 was the 12th workshop in the series. In 2006, the First International Workshop on ISI (WISI) was held in Singapore in conjunction with the Pacific Asia Conference on Knowledge Discovery and Data Mining (PAKDD 2006). The workshop attracted over 100 contributors and participants from all over the world and marked the start of a new series of ISI meetings in the Pacific Asia region. In the following few years, the workshop was held in Chengdu, China (2007), Taipei, Taiwan (2008), Bangkok, Thailand (2009), Hyderabad, India (2010), Beijing, China (2011, 2013), Kuala Lumpur, Malaysia (2012), Tainan, Taiwan (2014), Ho Chi Minh City, Vietnam (2015), and Auckland, New Zealand (2016). This year, the Pacific Asia ISI Workshop series (PAISI 2017) was once again held in conjunction with PAKDD 2017 in Jeju, South Korea.

PAISI 2017 brought together ISI researchers from Pacific Asia and other regions working on a variety of fields and provided a stimulating forum for them to exchange ideas and report on their research progress. The one-day program included a keynote speech and presentations of eight long and one short papers, covering such topics as information access and security, cybersecurity and infrastructure protection, data and text mining, and network-based data analytics. We wish to express our sincere gratitude to all workshop Program Committee members, who provided valuable and constructive review comments.

March 2017

Alan Wang
Michael Chau
Hsinchun Chen

Organizing Committee and Program Committee

Workshop Co-chairs

G. Alan Wang — Virginia Tech, USA
Michael Chau — The University of Hong Kong, SAR China
Hsinchun Chen — The University of Arizona, USA

Program Committee

Weiping Chang	Central Police University, Taiwan
Xueqi Cheng	Chinese Academy of Sciences, China
Vlad Estivill-Castro	Griffith University, Australia
Uwe Glässer	Simon Fraser University, Canada
Daniel Hughes	Massey University, New Zealand
Eul Gyu Im	Hanyang University, South Korea
Da-Yu Kao	Central Police University, Taiwan
Siddharth Kaza	Towson University, USA
Paul Kwan	University of New England, USA
Wai Lam	The Chinese University of Hong Kong, SAR China
Mark Last	Ben-Gurion University of the Negev, Israel
Ickjai Lee	James Cook University, Australia
Xin Li	City University of Hong Kong, SAR China
Hsin-Min Lu	National Taiwan University, Taiwan
Xin Luo	University of New Mexico, USA
Byron Marshall	Oregon State University, USA
Dorbin Ng	The Chinese University of Hong Kong, SAR China
Shaojie Qiao	Southwest Jiaotong University, China
Srinath Srinivasa	International Institute of Information Technology, Bangalore, India
Aixin Sun	Nanyang Technological University, Singapore
Paul Thompson	Dartmouth College, USA
Harry Wang	University of Delaware, USA
Jau-Hwang Wang	Central Police University, Taiwan
Jennifer Xu	Bentley University, USA
Liao You-Lu	Central Police University, Taiwan
Yilu Zhou	Fordham University, USA

Contents

Cybersecurity and Infrastructure Protection

The Cyberbullying Assessment of Capable Guardianship in Routine Activity Theory

Da-Yu Kao, Benjamaporn Kluaypa, and Hung-Chih Lin[✉]

Department of Information Management, Central Police University,
Taoyuan City 333, Taiwan, ROC
xlunalay@gmail.com

Abstract. Cyber world is undergoing constant and boundless development when cybercrime has always hindered its progress. The advantages of digitalization has inevitably enabled crime to expand its unhindered impact by physical limitations. As the Internet becomes accessible, cyberbullying inflicts social and mental wounds upon the victims. As the presence of cyberbullying becomes more prominent, awareness must be raised among Internet users of its insidious nature. If an individual is exposed to a criminally infested environment in his everyday lifestyle, there is a high possibility for him/her to conform to criminal behaviors and activities. Implications for Routine Activity Theory (RAT) are discussed in Taiwan cyberbullying incident. It is believed that the proposed capable guardianship strategy can protect Internet users from being victimized by cyberbullying, facilitate to cut down its circuit, and fight against it.

Keywords: Routine activities theory · Capable guardianship · Cyberbullying

1 Introduction

1.1 Cyberbullying Depression as a Risk Factor for Suicide

The modus operandi of cyberbullying could be described below [7]: Cyberbullies often prey upon potential victims by sending an e-mail to the targets, or engage in a petty disagreement in the online forums or chat rooms. These enable them to attack the victims directly. Threats, hints of sexual harassment, hate speeches, or blackmailing comments are directed towards the victims to make them lose Internet prestige, credibility, or even push them towards a nervous breakdown. Cyberbullying affects people of all ages, from children, adolescents, to adults, and can occur at any place and time [16]. The impact of cyberbullying does not limit to only within the Cyber world. Fear, paranoia, depression, and the feeling of inescapability are also forced upon the victims in real life. They seek any possible means to grant themselves respite from the negativity, including suicide [10]. Upon being exposed to cyberbullying, different individuals may be affected on different levels. Among potential effects, depression is perceived as a risk factor for suicidal behavior. For female victims, cyber victimization is strongly related to depression [1]. Females are more emotionally affected, possess a self-centric way of thinking, and have a high tendency to draw up an imaginary audience. The perceived appearance

G.A. Wang et al. (Eds.): PAISI 2017, LNCS 10241, pp. 3–14, 2017.
DOI: 10.1007/978-3-319-57463-9_1

of the imaginary audience may contribute to the development of depression, in which the female victims magnify the belief that the entire world is aware of their humiliation.

Many cyberbullying actions attempt to damage friendships, social status, or reputation. Cyberbullying is one of onerous topics. Cyberbullying victimization rates have increased from 18.8 percent in 2007 to 33.6 in 2016 [17]. According to the Cyberbullying Research Center in the USA survey of 2,000 middle schools, findings are listed as follow [9]:

- 20% respondents seriously thought about suicide.
- 19% respondents have attempted suicide.
- Cyberbullying victims were 1.9 times more likely to attempt suicide than non-victims.

1.2 Cyberbullying on Social Media

In the past, people often engage social interaction in private. However, the emergence of social media platform has evolved social interaction into an expansive network with multiple contacts. This enables simultaneous social interactions and relationship bonding among Internet users [12]. Cyberbullying victimization is related to the frequency of Internet usage, the number of Internet contacts, and the duration spent on social networks. Social media platforms are often where Internet abuse occur. Two of the most prominent cyberbullying platforms are Facebook and Twitter [14]. Online behaviors that pose a risk of victimization to the users is revealing private information and befriending strangers [11]. Revealing one's private information renders the users vulnerable and exposable to cyberbullying actions. The American Megan Meier foundation also found the following issues [13]:

- 90% of teens have witnessed cyberbullying on social media.
- 72% of teens are cyberbullied once or twice during the school year.
- 71% of teens use more than one social network, and come across cyberbullying in some shapes or forms.
- 42% of teens are cyberbullied in the past year.
- 21% of teens check social media to assure nobody was saying something about them.

The literature reviews about cyberbullying explanation and Routine Activity Theory (RAT) are described in Sect. 2. This paper has conducted to test this theory from the viewpoint of cyberbullying lifestyle. Section 3 takes a Taiwanese cyberbullying case as an example, and examines the RAT application to fight against it. The capable guardianship strategy is proposed in Sect. 4. Our conclusion is drawn in Sect. 5.

2 Literature Reviews

2.1 Bullying and Cyberbullying

2.1.1 Bullying

Bullying is defined as an aggressive behavior that includes three basic components: intention to cause harm, repetition, and power imbalance [16]. Bullying involves direct or indirect aggression. Face-to-Face (FTF) bullying can be accomplished physically, verbally or relationally. Direct aggression includes physical and verbal bullying. Physical bullying involves hitting, kicking, or pushing someone [6]. Verbal bullying involves malicious teasing, name calling, and insults. It can be based on one's appearance, belief, or perceived difference. Relational bullying involves the use of rumor-mongering and gossiping. The falsified or private information of the victims are spread around behind their back [20]. Bullying carries a malicious intent to hurt a lower-hand person in order to gain a sense of superiority and power. This in turn causes the victims to feel oppressed and helpless [11].

2.1.2 Cyberbullying

There is no broadly-accepted definition of cyberbullying due to the inconsistencies of harassment in cyberspace. Cyberbullying can be defined as aggression, harm, social exclusion, insults, humiliation, or threats to one's physical and mental safety [9]. Cyberbullying is one type of cyber harassment against individuals, and is grouped in the subcategory of non-sexual crime as emotional injuries [8]. Cyberbullying is defined as "an aggression that is repeatedly and intentionally carried out through electronic media (e.g., email, instant message, social networking sites, and text messages) [10]." In 2008, Jaishankar defines cyberbullying as "abuse/harassment by teasing or insulting victims' body, shape, intellect, family background, dress sense, mother tongue, place of origin, attitude, race, caste, class, name calling, using modern telecommunication networks [8]." Cyberbullying tends to occur on any social media platform. Three characteristics of cyberbullying are listed as follow: (1) intention (2) lack of power balance between an aggressor and a victim, and (3) repetition through communicative technologies [18]. Cyberbullying is used to intimidate, harass, victimize or bully an individual or a group of individuals.

2.1.3 Comparison

Bullying and cyberbullying are arguably excessively used among adults and children [19]. These two aggression acts repeatedly occur over the course of individuals' relationship. Their divergences in Table 1 include appearance, duration, witness, and motives [3, 7, 14].

Table 1. The different forms of bullying and cyberbullying

Features	Bullying	Cyberbullying
Appearance	Face-to-face	Identity imitation or anonymous
Duration	Working time	Any time
Witness	Small	Large
Motives	Initial power and advantage	Avenge

Appearance. One reason for Internet users to commit cyberbullying is the effortlessness of identity falsification and anonymity [14]. Internet users tend to remain anonymous, and feel a sense of detachment from the consequence of cyberbullying. While bullying offenders either know their victims personally or are familiar with them, cyberbullies conceal their identities by remaining anonymous. Cyberbullying offenders can imitate and cover their identities by pretending to be another person. They would be reluctant to do so in real life.

Duration. Most bullying occurs during office hours or school period. However, cyberbullying is not restricted to certain periods and can occur at any time. High accessibility of social contact and constant interaction allows offenders to prey on the victims at any place and time. While on certain occasions, victims decide to shut down their accounts or cease to attend the virtual forums in which their negative information is posted, the fact that these information can still be perceived by other people remains.

Witness. The witness or audience of bullying is small and limited to people within perceivable distance, while the group of cyberbullying audience can be large or global on the Internet. Some of the witnesses have been subjected to cyberbullying.

Motives. The difference between cyberbullying and bullying is the goal [7]. Bullying usually has an objective on attaining initial power, and takes advantage over their victims. Cyberbullying, however, may occur because of several reasons, from taking revenge for disagreement over the Internet to simply attempting self-gratification through dominance and display of power.

2.2 Routine Activity Theory

Routine Activity Theory (RAT) states that the following three specific criteria must be involved for a committed crime: a motivated offender, a suitable target, and the absence of a capable guardian [23]. RAT focuses on criminal inclination, and explains the victim's involvement. It focuses on how daily routine activities or lifestyles of individuals create opportunities for offenders. In Fig. 1, crime occurs when there is the convergence of three elements in proper time and space. The convergence of these three elements creates opportunities for criminal activities to occur, and increases the likelihood of victimization. The nonexistence of any of the three elements can result in the prevention of the crime. Individuals' daily routine activities influence the risk of victimization, and the chance of coming into contact with the offenders [5]. The increase in crime rate does not result in the increase in the number of offenders, but the increase in the windows of opportunity accessible to the offenders [22].

2.2.1 Motivated Offenders

A person who is likely to commit a crime may be anyone with a motive and the capacity to do so [4]. A motivated offender may not always have a chance to commit a crime. The decision to commit a crime may vary, and is based on the factors surrounding each motivated offender.

Fig. 1. The convergence of three elements from RAT

2.2.2   Suitable Targets

A suitable target is a person or property that may be threatened by an offender. The target of harassment is also called "victim." The probability of a suitable target can be described by the risk level of VIVA (Value, Inertia, Visibility, and Access). The target suitability of individuals in the virtual world is more active than the physical world [22]. The target can be globally exposed to criminals in the virtual world. The physical distance between the motivated offenders and the suitable targets becomes non-existent. Online users set up their interested lifestyles by participating in various communities [3]. One of the key factors that makes up a suitable target is their vocational or leisure activities.

2.2.3   Absence of Capable Guardianship

A capable guardian can intervene to stop or impede a crime [4]. The absence of capable guardianship shows up when crime occurs. Capable guardians should not be limited to individuals within the law enforcement institutions alone. The physical or symbolic presence of an individual either in direct or indirect relation to the potential victim might deter a potential criminal event, or even protect the target from being victimized. Any capable guardian, who moves through an area or who functions as a guard assigned to the persons or properties, is also included in RAT.

3   Case Study

3.1   Suicide Case

This cyberbullying case occurred in April 2015 to a 24-year-old Taiwan entertainer named "Cindy Yang." Cindy was known from her frequent appearance on TV show programs, variety shows and movies. Cindy committed suicide in her residence at Taichung, and left a suicide note on her body. The note contained critical information pertaining to her cyber victimization, and the desire to push the insidious nature of cyberbullying into the spotlight through her death. Prior to her suicide, Cindy encountered various problems: She became a social pariah among her peers, was heavily disappointed with her work, and had a rough time dealing with cyberbullying. She strived to do the right thing, but the result turned out badly. Combined with insomnia, professional pressure, and occasional visits to various hospitals for mental disorder, Cindy was unable to cope with the ongoing online libel and slander. Her emotional instability was used as ammunition against her.

Several hate induced posts on Facebook did not directly mention Cindy, but instead used Chinese characters that are homonymous with the name "Cindy Yang". It is apparent that the posts are targeted at Cindy, calling out on her phoniness, naivety, hypocrisy, and so on. One particular Facebook fan page called "Kao Bei Bloggers" regularly attacked Cindy's character through hateful messages. Cindy thought that the people behind these attacks were her friends, which made her upset and had no idea who she could trust. She had tried to reply many of the posts and showed her intolerance of such blatant cyberbullying. All of her efforts were to no avail. Eventually, Cindy left a message blessing her followers on her fan page before the day of her suicide.

3.2   Discussions and Analyses

If an individual is exposed to a criminally infested environment in his everyday lifestyle, there is a high possibility for him to conform to criminal behaviors and activities. Individuals' daily routine activities and lifestyles create situations or opportunities for offenders to commit crimes [15]. Implications for Routine Activity Theory (RAT) are discussed and analyzed in Fig. 2.

3.2.1   Motivated Offenders
Personal Profile. The personal profile can identify a person's friends, family members, and associates [12]. Most sites, such as Facebook, support the creation of explicit social connections with other users. Such social connections tend to come in two forms: friending and following. These personal profiles imply that individuals would like to interact with others. Motivated offenders know about the victim by gaining access to her social media profiles.

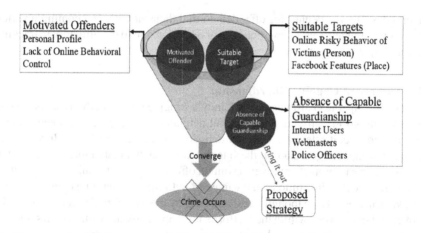

Fig. 2. The observation on cindy case

Lack of Online Behavioral Control. Some users joined the cyberbullying, and their behaviors were not well-controlled. The lack of behavioral control encouraged individual participation in criminal activity [2]. Motivated offenders will place themselves in close proximity with the targets.

3.2.2 Suitable Targets

Certain factors make people suitable targets for cyberbullying. Victims can be exposed to offenders when their personal information can be easily accessed on the Internet or social media platforms through popular search engines. These user demographics can be easily accessed by any Internet user, as they are essential in helping individuals connect with friends. This had led the offenders to come into contact with Cindy and began their attacks.

Online Risky Behaviors of Victims (Person). With the emergence of social media platforms and detailed personal profiles, it is easy for cyber offenders to piece together personal information of the prime victims. Victims, who post personal information on blogs or write journals about sensitive issues, may be easy targets for offenders to exploit their emotional vulnerabilities. Such sensitive issues include: deepest desires, likes/dislikes, real-time moods, pictures, addresses, and phone numbers. Cindy was a well-known entertainer. To connect with her fans, she had to create her own Facebook page to allow public access to her identity. The risk of cyber victimization was increased due to individuals' online risky behavior on social media [2]. Cindy's risky decision to grant public access to her profile had inevitably turned her into a suitable target.

Facebook Features (Place). A suitable target can include a person, an object, or a place. Internet users make use of the various communication tools, such as public forums, chat rooms, and instant messaging application. Peer to peer communication inevitably provides an opportunity for cyberbullying, and increases the possibility of users becoming targets of cyber victimization [21]. In Cindy's case, Facebook is a platform that facilitates suitable venues for offenders to find their victims, and commit a variety of offenses without any fear of consequence or detection due to the difficulty in tracking, apprehending, or prosecuting cyber criminals [23].

3.2.3   Absence of Capable Guardianship

The absence of capable guardians during Cindy's struggle with cyberbullying is notable. In the physical world, a friendly and helpful neighborhood, law enforcement officers, or even closed-circuit televisions can be defined as capable guardians. However, the definition of a capable guardian on the Internet is somewhat disputable. While certain guardians are able to protect or prevent criminal offenses within the online society, there is no prominent cyber institutions that can exert authority or claim responsibility over the vast virtual space. Even though Facebook employ the use of moderators to supervise the movement of the users within the platform, it is apparently not sufficient in screening and maintaining a safe space and appropriate contents for everyone. As Cindy was a public figure, she could not avoid engaging in online activities. She was therefore exposed to cyber victimization. Nevertheless, capable guardianship remains an essential key in fighting and preventing cyberbullying. Online capable guardianship can be identified as the following three types: internet users, webmasters, and police officers.

Internet Users. The population of Facebook users continuously increases. Capable guardians are users who witnessed the cyberbullying occurrences on various Facebook pages. They can be either Cindy's Facebook friends or followers.

Webmasters. Webmasters are the head administrators of the respective social media platform, and can act as guardians to supervise over the forum.

Police Officers. A police officer has authority to investigate, suppress or prevent crimes. However, in Cindy's case, no report was filed to the police force.

4   A Purposed Capable Guardianship Strategy for Fighting Cyberbullying

Capable guardians can prevent and discourage potential offenders from perpetrating the crimes. The absence of capable guardianship allows offenders free reign over the virtual space and renders the users vulnerable to their malicious attacks. However, a criminal act may not be accomplished if the space is well guarded [23]. In the physical world, law enforcement officers and neighbors act as guardians that can monitor the compound. The use of Closed-Circuit Television (CCTV) can also help house owners watch the house's premise and surroundings. In the Cyber world, there are three elements that constitute capable guardianship: Police officers (Law enforcement agents), Internet users (Neighbors), and Webmasters (Community leader). This proposed capable guardianship strategy is based on the 'Nip in the bud' concept which builds the collaboration between Internet users, law enforcement and all members of communities or organizations to prohibit the threat of cyberbullying. It comprises the obligation, alert, and preventive in Table 2.

Table 2. Fighting cyberbullying strategy through capable guardianship

	Physical capable guardianship		
Nip in the bud	Internet Users (Neighborhood)	Webmasters (Community leader)	Police Officers (Law Enforcement Agents)
Obligation	Cyber-surrounding monitory	Terms of use	Framework development
Alert	Warning attention	Red box in risky place	Online patrol
Preventive	Primary report	Negative point deletion	Stop cyberbullying Campaign

4.1   Internet Users

Individuals can come together with police officers to implement an online community watch program. Internet users can help prevent crime by posting crime alerts, and raise awareness of suspicious cyberbullying activities in their surrounding areas. This enables them to report cyberbullying and suspicious activity to other Internet users, webmasters, or police officers in real time.

4.1.1   Cyber-Surrounding Monitory
Crime and the fear of crime create special issues on the Internet. Cyberbullying prevention is not the duty of police officers alone, but every user's duty [4]. Internet users have a small but significantly desirable impact in combating cyberbullying. All users should act as good neighbors and keep a keen eye on the social interactions inside the virtual world.

4.1.2   Warning Attention
Crime preventive measures help online users create a safe and secure social space [3]. An alert system that warns against and blocks any message with malicious intent can help filter much of the negativity that permeates the atmosphere of the interaction. Documenting evidence of the crime can make it difficult for criminals to commit cyberbullying and retain their anonymity. Whenever a cyberbullying occurs, a witness can help capture evidence from messages or pictures to prosecute the offender in the near future.

4.1.3   Primary Report
Cyberbullying messages can usually be screen captured and presented to someone who has the authority to help. If someone detects any cyberbullying conflict or possibility, reporting the incident to webmasters or police officers will be essential in narrowing down the

offenders and removing the threat [14]. Webmasters are equivalent to that of the landlords and are obligated to take care of his or her villagers whenever an offense occurs.

4.2 Webmasters

Webmaster is the community leader or landlord, who is perceived to represent the community and has responsibility for looking after all members' safety. In case of criminal occurrence in physical world, police who has built up a familiarity with the leader will identify and solve problems effortlessly.

4.2.1   Terms of Use

The terms of use provide a rule or regulation for webmasters to ban cyberbullying in good order [12]. Each type of cyberbullying incident differs in motives, solutions and responses. There is no golden rule that fits all when cyberbullying is concerned. Preventing cyberbullying can be initiated from educating the Internet users about the consequences of account suspension or permanent ban. Users should respect others and take a stand against cyberbullying.

4.2.2   Red Box in Risky Place

"Red box" normally appears at many places where is considered as a risky place. Inside the red box is contained a notebook which a patrol police will sign in while patrolling. People can drop the comments about suspicious incident into the box either [6]. Red box is set up for decreasing the occurrence of crime in community. Crime hubs in cyberspace are socializing sites including online chat rooms, blogs, public message boards, social networking sites, and online dating sites [8]. Red box in this proposed strategy means a website could send a warning to all users or allow them to report any incident directly into it. This function also allows relevant authorities (ex. webmasters) to notify the information to members independently.

4.2.3   Negative Point Deletion

When a user becomes aware of any post, message, and comment with the clear intent to start cyberbullying, website administrators can remove them permanently and prevent the crime from occurring in the first place.

4.3 Police Officers

This strategy presents the community-based crime prevention by utilizing neighborhood surveillance, police building ties with communities' members, and the principle of patrol police duty. Interactive partnership and collaboration are created for developing problem-solving solutions.

4.3.1   Framework Development

Law enforcement officers are obligated to develop a framework for crime investigation or crime prevention [15]. Crime prevention means being aware of online environment and remaining alert to risky situations that could make users vulnerable to crime. Previous cyberbullying cases could be examined to gather crime determinants, offender's behaviors, and victims' weakness.

4.3.2   Online Patrol

Online patrols can create protection, alert the community, and safeguard users inside the cyberspace [23]. Any incident will be reported without delay. Police officers need to cover their identities, keep a low profile, and reveal as little information as possible. Social media allows users to post any message or comment anonymously. These sites are risky places for cyberbullying, and police officers should constantly keep monitoring their actions on the Internet.

4.3.3   Stop Cyberbullying Campaign

The Stop Cyberbullying campaign protects victims by preventing sharing, or participation in the offense [23]. Police officers can promote the campaign on the organization's website or spread the awareness to various communities with the cooperation from media, academic institutions and leader of the communities.

5   Conclusion

Routine Activity Theory (RAT) is analyzed in the Taiwan's Cindy cyberbullying incident. Motivated offenders can gain access to victims' personal information with lack of online behavioral control. Cindy became a suitable target due to her online risky behaviors (person) and Facebook features (place). The "nip in the bud" strategy includes the obligation, alert and preventive action. Capable guardians could be police officers, Internet users and webmasters. An increase in guardianship roles has a positive effect on the reduction of cyberbullying offenses. Future study will work on another two variants, motivated offenders and suitable targets, to fight against cyberbullying efficiently. Cyberbullying could possibly change into an aggressive crime in nature if left unchecked. People should be made aware of the threats of cyberbullying and help each other in safeguarding and spreading knowledge in the community.

References

1. Cash, S.J., Bridge, J.A.: Epidemiology of youth suicide and suicidal behavior. Curr. Opin. Pediatr. **21**(5), 613–619 (2009)
2. Choi, K.S.: Computer crime victimization and integrated theory: an empirical assessment. Int. J. Cyber Criminol. **2**(1), 308–333 (2008)
3. Choi, K.S.: Cyber Criminology and Digital Investigation. LFB Scholarly Publishing LLC, El Paso (2015)

4. Cohen, L.E., Felson, M.: Social change and crime rate trends: a routine activity approach. Am. Sociol. Rev. **44**, 588–608 (1979)
5. Cohen, L.E., Kluegel, J.R., Land, K.C.: Social inequality and predatory criminal victimization: an exposition and test of a formal theory. Am. Sociol. Rev. **46**, 505–524 (1981)
6. Crick, N.R., Bigbee, M.A.: Relational and overt forms of peer victimization: a multi informant approach. J. Consult. Clin. Psychol. **66**(2), 337–347 (1998)
7. Feinberg, T., Robey, N.: Cyberbullying. Principal Leadersh. (Middle School Edition) **9**(1), 10–14 (2008)
8. Halder, D., Jaishankar, K.: Cyber Crime and the Victimization of Women: Laws, Rights and Regulations. Information Science Reference. IGI Global, Pennsylvania (2012)
9. Hinduja, S., Patchin, J.W.: Bullying, Cyberbullying, and Suicide. Arch. Suicide Res. **14**(3), 206–221 (2010)
10. Kowalski, R.M., Limber, S.P., Agatston, P.W.: Cyberbullying: Bullying in the Digital Age, 2nd edn. Wiley-blackwell, Malden (2012)
11. Kwan, G.C.E., Skoric, M.M.: Facebook bullying: an extension of battles in school. Comput. Hum. Behav. **29**(1), 16–25 (2013)
12. Maar, M.C.: An Examination of Organizational Information Protection in The Era of Social Media – A Study of Social Network Security and Privacy Protection. Proquest LLC, Michigan (2013)
13. Malcore, P.: Teen Cyberbullying and Social Media Use on the Rise [INFOGRAPHIC]. Rawhide Boys Ranch, pp. 1–8 (2015)
14. Marcum, C.D., Higgins, G.E.: Social Networking as a Criminal Enterprise. CRC Press, Florida (2014)
15. Miethe, T.D., Meier, R.F.: Crime and its Social Context: Toward an Integrated Theory of Offenders, Victims, and Situations. State University of New York Press, Albany (1994)
16. Olweus, D.: Bullying at School: What We Know and What We Can Do. Blackwell Publishing, Malden (1993)
17. Patchin, J.W.: Summary of Our Cyberbullying Research (2004–2016), Cyberbullying Research Center, pp. 1–2 (2016)
18. Ong, R.: Cyber-bullying and young people: how Hong Kong keeps the new playground safe. Comput. Law Secur. Rev. **31**(5), 668–678 (2015)
19. Sabella, R.A., Patchin, J.W., Hinduja, S.: Cyberbullying myths and realities. Comput. Hum. Behav. **29**(6), 2703–2711 (2013)
20. Tsaousis, I.: The relationship of self-esteem to bullying perpetration and peer victimization among schoolchildren and adolescents: a meta-analytic review. Aggress. Violent. Beh. **31**, 186–199 (2016)
21. Wolak, J., Finkelhor, D., Mitchell, K.J., Ybarra, M.L.: Online "Predators" and their victims: myths, realities and implications for prevention and treatment. Am. Psychol. **63**(2), 111–128 (2008)
22. Yar, M.: The novelty of cybercrime: an assessment in light of routine activities theory. Eur. J. Criminol. **2**(4), 407–427 (2005)
23. Yucedal, B.: Victimization in Cyberspace: An Application of Routine Activity and Lifestyle Exposure Theories. Doctoral Dissertation, Kent State University Institute of Philosophy (2010)

The Hierarchy of Cyber War Definitions

Daniel Hughes[✉] and Andrew Colarik

Massey University, Palmerston North, New Zealand
daniel.hughes.1@uni.massey.ac.nz, a.m.colarik@massey.ac.nz

Abstract. With the advent of militaries declaring cyberspace as the fifth domain of military warfare, those modern societies that are heavily dependent on its reliable operation need to have a clear understanding of the actors and future activities brought about by this new doctrine. Knowing what is meant by the terms 'cyber war' and 'cyber warfare' is critical to navigating a path forward in preparing for and mitigating the effects caused by such activities. In this paper, the authors identified and analysed 159 documents containing the definitions for these terms in order to discern definitional origins, patterns of usage and the relative trends that emerge as a result. From this analysis, we construct a discourse hierarchy of cyber war and cyber warfare definitions, both as a representation of the findings as well as a basis for incorporating future works into the larger context of the domain.

Keywords: Cyber · War · Warfare · Discourse analysis · Definition · Hierarchy

1 Introduction

Cyberspace is a global Information and Communications Technology (ICT) infrastructure that has rapidly evolved and expanded to become an integral component of modern society. It has facilitated immense increases in the range, reach and volume of communications on a scale never seen before. Cyberspace enables mass communication, global supply chains, shared intelligence, and access to the ideas of a diverse set of cultural norms and customs. Its continued persistence is now integral to everyday life and the functioning of modern States and the broader international system. As a result, cyberspace has attained a strategic significance with both national and international dimensions.

The strategic value of cyberspace rests both in the infrastructure itself and in the information that is being globally stored, transmitted, and shared. This massive infrastructure moves across State borders – sovereign areas of controlled space. It also traverses those expanses that are open to all nations; international waters and orbital pathways. The data and information flowing through this infrastructure comprises many of the forms of communication that individuals, nation States and sub and supra State organizations use on a daily basis to conduct the transactions underpinning twenty first century society. Any deliberate disruption of this infrastructure or the information it contains is likely to be harmful to States, citizens, and international stability. Accordingly, governments across the world are expanding their security doctrines to include the defense - and in some cases the exploitation [1] - of cyberspace.

© Springer International Publishing AG 2017
G.A. Wang et al. (Eds.): PAISI 2017, LNCS 10241, pp. 15–33, 2017.
DOI: 10.1007/978-3-319-57463-9_2

Traditionally military doctrine considered land, sea, and air as operational domains of warfare. The advent of orbital and satellite technologies saw the addition of the operational domain of space. Now militaries have begun to consider cyberspace as the fifth domain of warfare. But just what does this mean? How does a military secure cyberspace? What weapons exist in their arsenal to defend it and what new weapons will need to be developed and deployed to do so? Over the years military scholars and academics have published a plethora of competing discussions envisioning cyber war, cyber warfare, and how best to prepare for it. However, in an initial exploration of military and academic literature pertaining to cyber war and cyber warfare, the authors discovered significant variations in how these terms have been defined. In an emerging field of study concerned with both the security and military exploitation of cyberspace - of such criticality to modern societies - the authors believe that definitions do matter. As such, we embarked on an extensive examination of competing definitions. Our aim was to better understand their uses, clarify their scope, and identify any patterns, categories and trends emerging from their application within the body of literature relevant to this domain. In the proceeding sections of the paper we articulate the methodological design used in selecting the body of literature, before providing a detailed analysis of our findings. We then used the results of our research to construct a discourse hierarchy of the definitions of cyber war and cyber warfare we have encountered. Finally, we present our conclusions and identify opportunities for future research.

2 Methodology

The methodological design of our examination was founded on the theory and practice of a social constructivist application of discourse analysis. Our methodology utilized the concept of an 'order of discourse' [2, 3], which we understand as a terrain in which competing discourses attempt to disseminate their claims to authoritative knowledge. In this case the competing discourses are the contrasting definitions of 'cyber war' and 'cyber warfare' that have been identified in the literature survey. Competition between discourses can be seen operating at two levels: textual – the competition between definitions set out in individual texts, and disciplinary, the competition between different academic disciplines. The texts upon which discourse analysis was performed were articles and papers that include the terms 'cyber war' or 'cyber warfare' in their title or abstract, as key words, or at least five times in the main body of text. Slight lexical variations of these terms, such as 'cyberwar', or 'cyber-war', were considered to be synonymous for the purposes of determining qualifying literature. Furthermore, to qualify as a text, a document must have been published on or before 31 July, 2016, and be either:

1. A peer reviewed article from an academic journal;
2. A peer reviewed paper from a published conference proceeding; or
3. A publicly available military document that has been published for internal or external use.

Use of Terms in Articles	Quantity
Cyber War Only	39
Cyber Warfare Only	43
Both terms, no distinction	75
Both terms, different definition	2
Total	159

Fig. 1. Use of terms in articles

The body of literature was generated through a series of searches on Google Scholar, using the terms cyber war, cyberwar, cyber-war, cyber warfare, cyberwarfare, and cyber-warfare. Qualifying articles were extracted from the first twenty pages of search results for each term. An important consideration of this approach was to ensure other scholars had the means to replicate and verify this process.

The key metrics extracted from each article for detailed analysis were definition, academic discipline, publication date, times cited, and terms used (e.g. cyber war or cyber warfare). In light of the diverse spectrum of cyber war and cyber warfare definitions we encountered, definitions were distilled into two categories – explicit and implicit. Definitions were considered explicit when an article presented a conception of cyber war or cyber warfare that was distinct, clearly stated, and unambiguous. The implicit definition category was used to group conceptions of cyber war and cyber warfare presented in the articles where an explicit definition of cyber war or cyber warfare was not present. Implicit definitions encompassed a wide spectrum of lingual specificity. This included uses of the term where a reasonably precise definition could be inferred from the text, through to uses of the terms in a 'purely descriptive, non-normative sense' [4] such as in The Tallinn Manual on the International Law Applicable to Cyber Warfare, through to uses of the terms that we regarded as largely superficial.

3   The Discourse of Definitions: Cyber War and Cyber Warfare

The research presented in this paper ultimately examined 159 publications as both a survey and a comparative analysis of definitions of cyber war and cyber warfare. We wish to emphasize that this was a descriptive, rather than a prescriptive activity. It was not our intent to argue for the indisputable validity of any one definition. Indeed, we believe that in a contested domain such efforts are more likely to confuse, rather than to clarify the discourse.

Our first task was to clarify the use of the terms cyber war and cyber warfare in discourse. We began with an assumption that differences between the terms could be understood by a traditional military distinction, where 'war' is held to be the act of war, while 'warfare' is the means. Accordingly, cyber warfare could be understood as the means of cyber war, and cyber war the act. However, this assumption was not borne out in our analysis. Figure 1 demonstrates the prevalence with which the terms were used in our methodological sample.

Tellingly, over half of the articles only used a single term in their analysis; 39 articles exclusively used 'cyber war' and 43 articles exclusively used 'cyber warfare'. 75 articles used both terms, but did not offer a means to formally distinguish between the terms. Only two articles offered distinct definitions of each term. Out of the 85 articles that made use of both terms 35 used cyber warfare as a dominant term, 20 used cyber war as a dominant term, while 20 articles used both terms with comparable frequency. The authors considered a term to be dominant if it was used at least twice as often as the competing term.

The authors did note that in 12 out of the 35 articles including both terms, with cyber warfare as the dominant term, that cyber war was used to denote a particular act or event, which aligned with our original assumption regarding the distinction between 'war' and 'warfare'. A similar pattern was used in articles that used both terms with comparable frequency; five out of 20 such articles used cyber war to indicate an act or event. While these trends are notable, we did not feel that they were of sufficient weight to alter the key conclusion we drew from this information – that the current discourse does not provide sufficient evidentiary basis to definitively distinguish between the terms cyber war and cyber warfare. In accordance with our descriptive analytical approach, we therefore concluded that the current state of the discourse necessitates that we consider cyber war and cyber warfare as synonymous terms. This is not to say that we believe this lack of distinction between the terms is desirable; indeed we regard the state of ambiguous equivalence between the terms as an impediment to focused research.

For our next task, we focused on the proportion of articles that offered a clearly stated explicit definition of cyber war or cyber warfare, versus articles that offered an implicit definition of cyber war or warfare. As illustrated in Fig. 2, out of the 159 articles examined we found that only 56 offered explicit definitions, versus 103 articles that based their analysis on generally weaker, implicit definitions of cyber war or warfare.

Explicit vs Implicit	Quantity
Explicit Defintions	56
Implict Defintions	103
Total	159

Fig. 2. Explicit vs. Implicit

The abundance of articles that base analysis on implicit rather than explicit definitions leads us to agree with the observations presented by Lewis [5] and Raboin [6], that ambiguous terminology weakens the analytical utility of the cyber war and warfare discourse. We further agree that the information we have uncovered lends credence to Liff's [7] observations, that '[W]ritings on cyberwarfare have long been plagued by major definitional problems, one consequence of which has been a lack of analytical coherence', and that the meaning of 'cyberwarfare' has become extremely convoluted in popular discourse. We do acknowledge that some articles instead offer an explicit definition of related terms such as 'cyber-attack' [4, 8], or 'cyber conflict' [9]. We believe, however, that unless the relationship of such ancillary terms to cyber war and cyber warfare is clearly articulated, the definition of further competing terms does little to clarify the discourse.

To develop a deeper understanding of the discourse we thought it essential to trace its emergence over time. Our sample begins in 1993 with Arquilla and Ronfeldt's seminal article 'Cyberwar is Coming!' [10]. Our data, shown in Fig. 3, illustrates that from the publication of Arquilla and Ronfeldt's article to the turn of the century, cyber war and cyber warfare discourse remained on the margins of academic debate. From 2000 until 2008 there was a gradual increase in the number of articles published. It was not, however, until 2009 that rapid growth in the discourse became evident. The number of articles published in the domain peaked in 2011, then remained strong through to 2013. From 2014 onwards there was a notable drop in the number of articles published.

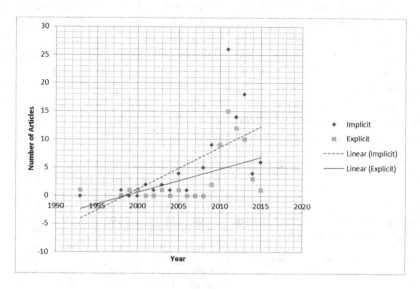

Fig. 3. Implicit/Explicit definitions by year

It is our contention that the number of articles published in the discourse peaks in response to what we consider to be the three most notable cyber incidents in the international domain; the cyber conflicts between Russia and Estonia in 2007, between Russia and Georgia in 2008, and the Stuxnet attack in 2011. We believe that the 'lag' between the incidents of 2007 and 2008 and the marked increase in publications within the discourse can be attributed to the time taken for reliable information to emerge, in addition to the time required to take an article from conception through to publication in a peer reviewed conference or journal. Based on our observations of the waxing and waning of the discourse over time, we believe that the discourse will once again expand in response to further empirical incidents of cyber conflict. For example, while we believe that most researchers whose work we have studied would not consider the recent Russian cyber-attacks against the US Democratic Party and alleged interference in the 2016 US election as cyber war or warfare, we nonetheless believe that this event may generate a considerable body of academic work of relevance to the discourse of cyber war and warfare definitions.

As our survey of the cyber war and cyber warfare domain progressed, the inter-disciplinary nature of the discourse soon became apparent. As part of our analysis we categorized articles into different academic disciplines, based on the discipline the publication the article appeared in which it was most closely associated with. The results of this process are captured at Fig. 4. Four disciplines dominate the discourse: Information and Communication Technology (ICT), Law, Military Studies, and Strategic and Security studies. These four disciplines accounted for 133 out of the total 160 definitions encountered, and 47 out of the 57 explicit definitions. The remaining articles were grouped into the categories of International Relations, the International Conference on Cyber Conflict, and other. The International Conference on Cyber Conflict is hosted by the NATO Cooperative Cyber Defense Centre of Excellence (CCDOE) and includes submissions relevant to cyber security from a wide range of academic disciplines. Accordingly, the authors felt that articles published from conference proceedings could not accurately be categorized under a single academic discipline; indeed the diverse backgrounds of researchers participating in this conference is representative of the multi-disciplinary nature of the discourse. A similar conclusion can be drawn from the composition of the 'other' category, which includes articles from publications associated with International Management, Political Geography, and Philosophy.

Implicit/Explicit Definitions by Discipline					
Discipline	Implicit	Implicit %	Explicit	Explicit %	Total
Law	27.00	16.88%	14.00	8.75%	41.00
Military	22.00	13.75%	15.00	9.38%	37.00
Information and Communications Technology	22.00	13.75%	10.00	6.25%	32.00
Strategic Studies & Security Studies	15.00	9.38%	8.00	5.00%	23.00
Other	8.00	5.00%	3.00	1.88%	11.00
International Conference on Cyber Conflict	4.00	2.50%	4.00	2.50%	8.00
International Relations	5.00	3.13%	3.00	1.88%	8.00
Total	103.00	64.38%	57.00	35.63%	160.00

Fig. 4. Implicit/Explicit definitions by discipline

Out of the four dominant disciplines within the discourse, the largest body of work was associated with Law, with the majority of articles concerned with the implications that the emergence of cyber war and warfare will have on the existing Law of Armed Conflict, particularly the conditions under whether cyber war or warfare can be considered as a 'use of force', or 'armed attack'. The second largest body of work encountered in our sample was associated with ICT. We considered that this was the most fragmented discipline, both in the range of divergent positions advanced and the ambiguity with which the terms cyber war and warfare were used. While it included articles that we felt made valuable contributions to the discourse [5, 11], we also encountered articles where we considered the terms cyber war or cyber warfare were used with a significant degree of ambiguity and superficiality [12, 13].

The discipline of Military Studies made the third largest contribution of articles to the discourse. Unsurprisingly articles associated with the military discipline predominantly focused on how cyber war and warfare capabilities could be used to achieve military advantage. In addition, there discussion of the ramifications of cyber war and

Average Impact by Article			
Discipline	Implicit	Explicit	Total
Strategic Studies & Security Studies	39.70	128.00	84.00
Information and Communications Technology	48.18	26.90	37.54
Law	39.74	21.08	30.41
International Relations	16.60	27.67	26.30
Other	37.13	3.25	20.70
International Conference on Cyber Conflict	22.50	15.00	18.80
Military	16.73	18.27	17.70
Total	31.51	34.31	33.64

Fig. 5. Average impact by article

warfare for military ethics, ethos, and force development. Readers should note that this category includes publications from Military Law journals, which we included in the category because of our belief that their primary focus was on military, rather than purely legal matters.

The final dominant discipline we identified in the discourse relates to the fields of Strategic Studies and Security Studies. While these are usually thought of as distinct disciplines, they have similar fields of enquiry and are often published in venues that encompass both fields. For these reasons, we have elected to represent them as a single discipline for the purposes of our analysis. As could be expected, articles associated with this discipline placed much greater emphasis on the political, international, and strategic aspects of cyber war and cyber warfare.

To deepen our analysis, we then examined the influence of the articles associated with each discipline. Our measure of influence was the number of times an article had been cited. This data was extracted from Google Scholar during the collection of our sample in July and August 2016. We calculated the average citations per article in each discipline by adding together the total citations of each article, then dividing by the total number of articles in that discipline. This information was further broken down into average citations for both implicit and explicit definitions in each discipline.

As shown in Fig. 5, the most influential discipline in the discourse by citation count is Strategic and Security Studies, followed by ICT, Law, International Relations, Other, Cyber Conflict Conference, and finally, Military. However, if we discount citations from articles with implicit definitions, the rankings change to Strategic and Security Studies, International Relations, ICT, Law, Military, Cyber Conflict Conference, and Other. This allows us to draw several conclusions. Despite having the lowest number of articles out of the major disciplines active in the discourse, the fields of Strategic and Security Studies have had the greatest impact on the discourse. Conversely Military Studies, which has the second highest number of articles in our sample has had a low degree of influence on the discourse.

While the average citations count for articles featuring explicit definitions was slightly greater than that for articles featuring implicit definitions (34.31 to 31.51), we were surprised that this was not higher - we had assumed that articles with explicit definitions would be more influential in the discourse. In line with this observation we note that articles in the Law, ICT and Other categories with implicit definitions have been more influential than articles with explicit definitions. In the ICT category, we ascribe some of this phenomenon to an outlying article – Wang and Wang's 'Cyber Warfare: Steganography vs. Steganalysis' [12]. The large number of citations it has accrued (428) does not align with its limited relevance to the domain (cyber warfare is only mentioned once in the document), granting it a disproportionate weight in our calculations. If this outlier is removed the average citations for ICT articles with implicit definitions is reduced from 48.18 to 30.01, and the total average citations for all articles in with implicit definitions in our sample is reduced from 31.51 to 28.91. We have observed a similar pattern in the Other category, where two heavily cited articles with only ancillary discussion of cyber war and cyber warfare acted to inflate the average citation count for articles with implicit definitions.

The extent to which articles in the Law discipline with implicit definitions have exerted considerably greater influence than those with explicit definitions, is also worthy of further consideration. We contend this is due to a focus of the discipline, namely how cyber incidents should be conceived of with regard to The Law of Armed Conflict and International Humanitarian Law. More specifically, a substantial number of documents from the legal discipline consider the circumstances under which acts of cyber aggression should be considered as either a 'use of force', or an 'armed attack', as those terms are defined within the Charter of the United Nations. The majority of this type of analysis does not require a perennial definition of cyber war or warfare, as it is focused more on whether individual acts would cross thresholds established in international law.

4   Explicit Definitions of Cyber War and Cyber Warfare

Until this point our analysis had been focused on the totality of definitions we have encountered – both implicit and explicit. While consideration of implicit definitions has provided valuable information as to the shape of the discourse, we believed that further insight could be achieved through a more comprehensive analysis of the explicit definitions encountered in our survey. We began by more effectively ordering explicit definitions by consolidating duplicated definitions. We achieved this by counting each duplicate definition once, then associating it with the discipline of the article using that definition which had the highest citation count. This resulted in the total number of definitions being reduced from 57 to 44, as well as minor adjustments to the number of definitions associated with each discipline. The results of this process are illustrated in Fig. 6.

Our next action was to shift our analysis down to the level of individual explicit definitions, then to rank these according to influence (by citation count). The top five definitions are captured in Fig. 7.

Explicit Definitions (Duplicates Removed)		
Discipline	Explicit	%
Military	13	29.55%
Law	10	22.73%
Strategic Studies & Security Studies	7	15.91%
Information and Communications Technology	6	13.64%
International Conference on Cyber Conflict	3	6.82%
Other	3	6.82%
International Relations	2	4.55%
Total	44	100.00%

Fig. 6. Explicit definitions

Reference	Definition	Citations	Discipline
Arquilla, J., & Ronfeldt, D. (1993)	Cyberwar refers to conducting, and preparing to conduct, military operations according to information-related principles. It means disrupting, if not destroying, information and communications systems, broadly defined to include even military culture, on which an adversary relies in order to know itself: who it is, where it is, what it can do when, why it is fighting, which threats to counter first, and so forth. It means trying to know everything about an adversary while keeping the adversary from knowing much about oneself.	655	Strategic & Security Studies
Rid, T. (2012)	(Cyber) War has to have the potential to be lethal; it has to be instrumental; and it has to be political.	225	Strategic & Security Studies
Nicholson et al. (2012)	Attacks and defence issued by nation states take place over networks rather than by physical means	117	ICT
Schaap, A. J. (2009)	The use of network-based capabilities of one state to disrupt, deny, degrade, manipulate, or destroy information resident in computers and computer networks, or the computers and networks themselves, of another state	95	Law
Nye Jr, J. S. (2011)	Hostile actions in cyberspace that have effects that amplify or are equivalent to major kinetic violence	65	Military

Fig. 7. Top definitions by influence (citation count) [10, 14–17]

The five definitions listed in Fig. 7 have had the greatest influence by citation count out of individual articles encountered in our sample. As we have previously noted, however, we encountered several definitions that were repeated in several articles across several disciplines. While we regard this as further evidence of the cross-disciplinary nature of the cyber war and warfare discourse, we also believed that a more in depth examination of these 'cross-disciplinary definitions' provided another viable method to explore the influence of competing definitions. This led us to construct the table at Fig. 8, where we identified: (a) each cross-disciplinary definition; (b) the references for the articles in which the definition appeared; (c) the discipline of each article in which

Definition	Reference	Discipline	Citations	Original Source	Citations from Source	Total Citations
Cyberwar refers to conducting, and preparing to conduct, military operations according to information-related principles.	Cimbala, S. J. (2011).	Military	7	Arquilla, J., & Ronfeldt, D. (1993)	655	712
	Arquilla, J., & Ronfeldt, D. (1993).	Strategic & Security Studies	655			
	Liles et al. (2012)	Conference on Cyber Conflict	11			
	Reich et al.(2010)	Law	14			
	Arquilla, J. (2011).	IR	5			
Any act intended to compel an opponent to fulfil our national will, executed against the software controlling processes within an opponent's system.	Alford, L. D. (2000).	Military	9	Alford, L. D. (2000)	9	20
	Cahill, et al. (2003)	ICT	11			
"Cyber war is the uses of ICTs within an offensive or defensive military strategy endorsed by a state and aiming the immediate disruption or control of the enemy's resources. It is engaged with the informational environment, agents and targets ranging both on the physical and non-physical domains and level of violence completely depends on the situation	Taddeo, M. (2012)	Conference on Cyber Conflict	9	Taddeo, M. (2012)	9	13
	Ganji et al. (2013)	ICT	4			
The US Department of Defense defines a combined concept of computer network operations (CNO) as including CNA, computer network defence (CND) and computer network exploitation (CNE).	Leblanc et al. M. (2011)	ICT	12	US Department of Defence/ Joint Chiefs of Staff	130+	173+
	Chappelle et al. (2013).	Military	8			
	Kirsch, C. M. (2011).	Law	10			
	Turns, D. (2012).	Law	13			
Cyber war is the act of nation state to penetrate another nation's computer or network in order to cause damage or disruption.	Uma, M., & Padmavathi, G. (2013).	ICT	20	Clarke, R. A., & Knake, R. K. (2011)	792	830
	Saad et al. (2011).	ICT	5			
	Caplan, N. (2013).	Strategy & Security	4			
	Feil, J. A. (2012).	Law	5			
	Jolley, J. D. (2012).	Law	4			

Fig. 8. Breakdown of cross-disciplinary definitions [18–36]

the definition appeared; (d) the number of citations arising from each article; (e) the original source of the definition; (f) the citations arising from the source article; and (g) the total number of citations associated with the cross-disciplinary definition.

Out of the five cross-disciplinary definitions captured in Fig. 8, only the Arquilla and Ronfeldt definition is present in Fig. 7 - the initial table we constructed to demonstrate definition influence. We do note that Arquilla had modified his and Ronfeldt's original 1993 definition of cyber war (conducting military operations according to information related principles) to what may be considered a more modern formulation – 'An emergent mode of conflict enabled by and primarily waged with advanced information systems, which are in themselves both tools and targets' [21].

Out of the remaining four remaining cross-disciplinary definitions, we considered neither Alford's nor Taddeo's definitions to be sufficiently influential to warrant detailed analysis at that stage. Both definitions encountered were in only one other article and have generated minimal citations. Clarke and Knake's definition - 'Cyber war is the act of nation state to penetrate another nation's computer or network in order to cause damage or disruption' [36] - is succinct enough to require little explanation. Aside from its State-centric focus its most noteworthy point is the volume of citations it has generated – nearly 800. The background and context of the remaining cross-disciplinary definition – the concept of Computer Network Operations, promulgated by the US Department of Defense – is more complex and worthy of further explication.

Computer Network Operations (CNO) is a combined concept defined as consisting of Computer Network Attack (CNA), Computer Network Defence (CND) and Computer Network Exploitation (CNE). CNA is defined as '[a]ctions taken through the use of computer networks to disrupt, deny, degrade or destroy information resident in computers and computer networks, or the computers and networks themselves' [30]. CND is defined as '[a]ctions taken to protect, monitor, analyze, detect, and respond to unauthorized activity within the Department of Defense information systems and computer networks' [30]. CNE is defined as '[e]nabling operations and intelligence collection capabilities conducted through the use of computer networks to gather data from target or adversary automated information systems or networks' [30]. Notably, the Department of Defense source document does not explicitly equate CNO to cyber war or cyber warfare. However, this equation is made in the works of Turns [29], Kirsch [28], Leblanc et al. [26], and Chappelle et al. [27]. We regard the equivalence these authors assert between the terms CNO and cyber war or cyber warfare as valid, particularly when the concept of CNO is considered in light of the Department of Defense's (DoD) Strategy for Operating in Cyberspace [1]. Despite not making explicit use of the terms cyber war or cyber warfare, the strategy outlined in this document includes actions likely to be considered by many authors in the discourse as exemplary acts of cyber war or cyber warfare. For example the strategy notes how 'the President or the Secretary of Defense may determine that it would be appropriate for the U.S. military to conduct cyber operations to disrupt an adversary's military related networks or infrastructure' or to 'use cyber operations to terminate an ongoing conflict on U.S. terms'. Furthermore, the strategy notes how U.S. Cyber Command (USCYBERCOM) may be used 'to deter or defeat strategic threats in other domains', and sets a specific strategic goal that focuses on the creation and maintenance of cyber options to 'control conflict escalation and to shape the conflict environment at all stages' [1].

Neither of the original source documents from which the Clarke and Knake or US Department of Defense definitions arose were included in our sample. Clarke and Knake's definition was not originally published through an academic venue, while the source document for US Department of Defense's concept of Computer Network Operations was not returned in search results – presumably because it does not include the terms cyber war or cyber warfare. Our analysis shows, however, that both works have had considerable influence on the discourse. Indeed, as we have noted, Clarke and Knake's work has generated more citations than any other publication.

Based on our analysis of cross-disciplinary definitions we combined Fig. 7 – the most influential definitions by citation count from a single article, with Fig. 8 – the breakdown of cross-disciplinary definitions. The results are captured in Fig. 9. For reasons previously stated concerning low citations, we omitted Alford's 2000 definition and Taddeo's 2012 definition.

Figure 9 contains the seven most influential definitions that we encountered. However, under further analysis we regard only five of these as 'essential' or 'core' definitions, in that they ascribe cyber war or warfare certain characteristics or thresholds that cannot be deduced from other definitions. The five core definitions we have identified are Clarke & Knake [37], Arquilla and Ronfeldt [10], Rid [14], US Department of Defense [30], and Nye [17]. We contend that the definitions offered by Nicolson et al. [15] and Schaap [16] are more correctly viewed as being derived from the definitions offered by Clarke and Knake and the US Department of Defense. Both definitions utilize the State-centric conception of cyber war and cyber warfare found in Clarke and Knake, in addition to the emphasis on CNO that is the focus of the Department of Defense definition. We further justify this action by noting that Schaap's definition uses the language from the Department of Defense definition – 'the use of computer networks

Reference	Definition	Citations	Discipline
Clarke, R. A., & Knake, R. K. (2011)	Cyber war is the act of nation state to penetrate another nation's computer or network in order to cause damage or disruption.	830	N/A
Arquilla, J., & Ronfeldt, D. (1993)	Cyberwar refers to conducting, and preparing to conduct, military operations according to information-related principles. (1993)	655	Strategic & Security Studies
Rid, Thomas. (2012)	A potentially lethal, instrumental, and political act of force conducted through malicious code	225	Strategic & Security Studies
US Department of Defence (2010-2012)	Computer Network Operations (CNO) as including computer Network Attack (CNA), computer network defence (CND) and computer network exploitation (CNE).	173+	Military Studies
Nicholson et al. (2012)	Attacks and defence issued by nation states take place over networks rather than by physical means	117	ICT
Schaap, A. J. (2009)	The use of network-based capabilities of one state to disrupt, deny, degrade, manipulate, or destroy information resident in computers and computer networks, or the computers and networks themselves, of another state	95	Law
Nye Jr, J. S. (2011)	Hostile actions in cyberspace that have effects that amplify or are equivalent to major kinetic violence	65	Military

Fig. 9. Most influential definitions by citation count

to disrupt, deny, degrade or destroy information resident in computers and computer networks, or the computers and networks themselves' – verbatim.

5   A Discourse Hierarchy

Our analysis leads us to contend that the five core definitions we have identified form the foundations for a 'discourse hierarchy' of cyber war and cyber warfare definitions. We believe that out of the 44 explicit definitions we encountered in our analysis, 43 can be logically placed in the structure of our hierarchy. Each definition in the hierarchy either has a one to one relationship with a core definition. Alternatively, in cases where we have perceived that the definition in question included components from two distinct core definitions, a one to two relationship with two core definitions. Our discourse hierarchy is presented at Fig. 10. To explicate the underlying logic of the relationships within it, is necessary to expand upon each of the five core definitions that form its basis.

Rid's definition is presented in his provocatively titled article 'Cyber War Will Not Take Place'. Taking as his starting point the conception of war presented by Clausewitz [66], Rid states that cyber war is 'a potentially lethal, instrumental, and political act of force conducted through malicious code' [14]. This places an extremely high threshold on what would constitute cyber war or cyber war; indeed Rid argues 'that cyber war has never happened in the past, that cyber war does not take place in the present, and that it is unlikely that cyber war will occur in the future' [14]. No other authors we have encountered placed such demanding thresholds within their definition of cyber war or cyber warfare. However, a considerable number of definitions include sufficient components of Rid's definition to be grouped under him in the discourse hierarchy. Alford's 2000 definition, which we have previously encountered in our analysis of cross-disciplinary definitions, is a useful example. Alford's defines cyber warfare as 'any act intended to compel an opponent to fulfil our national will, executed against the software

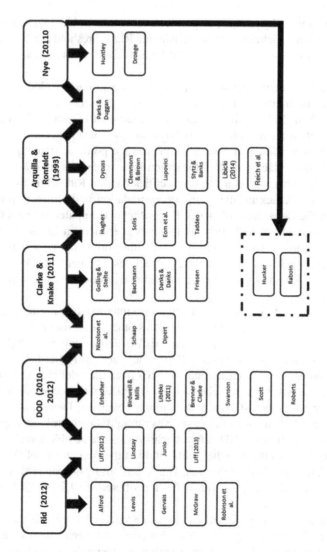

Fig. 10. Discourse hierarchy of cyber war and cyber warfare definitions [7, 15, 37–65]

controlling processes within an opponent's system.' [22] While it omits Rid's criterion of potentially lethal violence, we contend that this Alford's definition shares Rid's conception that cyber war and cyber warfare must involve an instrumental and political act of force. Lewis's 2012 definition – 'the use of cybertechniques to cause, damage, destruction, or casualties for political effect by States or political groups' [5] is in even closer alignment with Rid, although, in a similar manner to Alford, he stops short of saying that cyber war or cyber warfare must be potentially lethal. In addition, while one could argue that the concept of instrumentality is implicit in his definition, it is not an explicit threshold, as is the case with Rid. A final example is the definition offered by McGraw. In effect McGraw defines cyber war as the application of violent, physical force via virtual means by groups for 'political, economic, or ideological reasons' [38]. Once again McGraw's definition does not maintain Rid's threshold of potential lethality, but does emphasize that cyber war should be conceived of as a means to achieve a political end.

We consider the above definitions to have a one to one relationship with Rid's definition in the discourse hierarchy. There are other definitions, however, that utilize components of both Rid's definition and the Department of Defense's conception of CNO. An example is the definition offered by Junio [41], where cyber war is defined as a coercive act (using force to change or preserve a political status quo) involving Computer Network Attack (where information is disrupted, degraded, or destroyed). The emphasis on cyber war as a coercive act ties back to Rid, while the reference to Computer Network Attack and the disruption, degradation, or destruction of information is sourced from the Department of Defense's concept of Computer Network Operations. A similar combination of definition components is evident in Liff's 2012 definition where 'cyberwarfare is conceptualized as including only computer network attacks (CNA) with direct political and/or military objectives – namely, attacks with coercive intent and/or as a means to some strategic and/or brute force end – and computer network defense (CND)' [7].

While the above definitions are the result of the interaction of the definitions offered by Rid and the Department of Defense, numerous other definitions can be traced solely to the Department of Defense. Birdwell and Mills's define 'cyber war-fighting actions as CNA plus a subset of CND called CND-response actions (CND-RA)' [44], notably omitting Computer Network Exploitation (CNE) from their definition. A similar definition is offered by Scott et al.: 'Cyber warfare is typically associated with the fields of Computer Network Attack (CNA) and Computer Network Defense (CND)... CNA attempts to create tactical and strategic effects through the control and exploitation of network resources, whereas CND defends against these same objectives' [48]. Related definitions are observed through the combination of the Department of Defense definition and the Clarke and Knake definition. The definitions by Schaap [16] and Nicholson et al. [15] are useful examples; the definition offered by Dipert [50], is similarly comprised.

One of the key characteristics of Clarke and Knake's definition is that it stipulates cyber war and cyber warfare as something that occurs between nation states. The definitions located under Clarke and Knake within the hierarchy share this state-centric focus, albeit with slight variations. The definition offered by Golling and Stelte expands the scope of actors involved in cyber war and cyber warfare to include groups operating 'on behalf of, or in support of, a government' [51]. Danks and Danks's definition does not have a strict criterion that cyber war or warfare either originates from or is targeted at a State. Instead they state that 'cyberwarfare involves groups with the expertise and resources to mount a significant attack, including the accompanying research and development costs, and so arguably includes only those with the backing of a nation-state, whether the group is officially part of the state (e.g. military), or only sponsored (e.g., contractors), encouraged (e.g., patriotic hackers), or tolerated (e.g., international crime) by the state [53]. They further note that State backed groups 'typically have a goal that serves the interest of a particular State or state-like group' [53]. Conversely Bachmann's

2012 definition does not require that a specific category of actor initiates cyber war or cyber warfare, so long as the actor in question targets a State and has the means to launch 'a sustained campaign of concerted cyber operations' [52].

In a pattern similar to that observed elsewhere in the hierarchy, a number of definitions are constituted according to a dual relationship with both the Clarke and Knake and Arquilla and Ronfeldt definitions. Definitions such as those offered by Hughes [56], and Taddeo [24] utilize Arquilla and Ronfeldt's conception of cyber war and warfare – conducting military operations according to information-related principles – but add the additional criterion that cyber war and cyber warfare is 'waged by states and significant non-state actors' [56], or used 'within an offensive or defensive military strategy endorsed by a state' [24]. Other definitions grouped solely under Arquilla and Ronfeldt focus more exclusively on operational warfare and the furtherance of traditional, kinetic combat (see Libicki [63], Clemmons and Brown [60], and Lupovici [61]).

The final core definition within the hierarchy is that advanced by Nye – 'hostile actions in cyberspace that have effects that amplify or are equivalent to major kinetic violence' [17]. We regard Nye's definition as particularly useful as it provides a mechanism to group those definitions that make reference to the concepts of 'use of force' and 'armed attack', as they appear in international law. A considerable amount of the legal discourse pertaining to cyber war and cyber warfare discusses how these concepts, enshrined in the UN Charter, apply to cyber conflict. While there is considerable disagreement as to whether acts of cyber disruption can ever reach the threshold of the use of force, or even armed attack, there is near universal agreement that cyber war or warfare that causes physical destruction to a level equivalent to traditional kinetic weapons would cross these thresholds. Thus, within our hierarchy, we have aligned definitions such as those offered by Huntley [64], and Droege [65], with Nye's definition.

We have represented Hunker's 2012 definition [55] as the result of the combination of Nye's definition with that of Clarke and Knake, as he draws upon the latter's conception of cyber war as something that occurs between nation States. We have categorised Raboin's definition in a similar manner, as he states that 'cyber warfare … has come to symbolize a state sponsored use of weapons functioning within the cyberspace domain to create problematic and destructive real world effects' [6]. The final definition associated with Nye, that proposed by Parks and Duggan, has a relationship to Arquilla and Ronfeldt's definition. They state that 'cyber-warfare, is a combination of computer network attack and computer network defence' and that 'cyber warfare must have kinetic world effects' [11]. From the context of their paper 'The Principles of Cyber-warfare', we interpret this to primarily mean kinetic military effects.

6 Conclusions

Through our application of discourse analysis, we have deduced several conclusions regarding the nature of the discourse of cyber war and warfare definitions. First, the discourse provides no basis to definitively distinguish between the terms 'cyber war' and 'cyber warfare'; extensive synonymous use of the terms in the literature relevant to the domain precludes this. Second, despite location in a domain ostensibly concerned with the explication and implications of newly emerged technologies and modalities, a majority of articles do not offer explicit definitions of either cyber war or cyber warfare from which to base their analysis. Third, the expansion (and recession) of the discourse correlates with major international cyber incidents. Fourth, the discourse is inherently inter-disciplinary. This is demonstrated by the considerable bodies of research arising from publications associated with the disciplines of Information Communication Technology, Military Studies, Law, and Strategic and Security Studies. The inter-disciplinary nature of the discourse is further illustrated by the frequency with which definitions migrate across articles arising from different disciplines.

We have further concluded that the domain is characterized by both intra and inter-disciplinary competition between dozens of definitions, most of which have exerted minimal academic influence. While there are definitions that have been comparatively influential, there is no dominant functional definition of significance to the discourse. We contend that this is indicative of a domain contested by a multitude of stakeholders with differing agendas; and that this is a factor in the failure of the domain to produce a dominant functional definition.

While some element of fragmentation within the domain may be inescapable, we have nonetheless shown that almost all definitions we have encountered can be deduced from five core definitions - those identified through our application of discourse analysis methodology. The identification of these core definitions has in turn allowed us to construct a discourse hierarchy of cyber war and warfare definitions. While we believe that this hierarchy has value in its ability to represent a spectrum of disparate definitions under a single model, we have primarily constructed it in the hope that it may be expand upon and refined as the domain solidifies its use of definitions and associated outcomes.

References

1. Department of Defense. DoD Cyber Strategy (2015). http://www.defense.gov/Portals/1/features/2015/0415_cyberstrategy/Final_2015_DoD_CYBER_STRATEGY_for_web.pdf. Accessed
2. Jørgensen, M.W., Phillips, L.J.: Discourse Analysis as Theory and Method. Sage, London (2002)
3. Fairclough, N.: Critical Discourse Analysis: The Critical Study of Language (1995)
4. Schmitt, M.N.: Tallinn Manual on the International Law Applicable to Cyber Warfare. Cambridge University Press, Cambridge (2013)
5. Lewis, J.: Cyberwar thresholds and effects. IEEE Secur. Priv. **9**(5), 23–29 (2011)
6. Raboin, B.: Corresponding evolution: international law and the emergence of cyber warfare. J. Nat. Assoc. Adm. Law Judiciary **31**, 602 (2011)
7. Liff, A.P.: Cyberwar: a new 'absolute weapon'? The proliferation of cyberwarfare capabilities and interstate war. J. Strateg. Stud. **35**(3), 401–428 (2012)
8. Nguyen, R.: Navigating jus ad bellum in the age of cyber warfare. Cal. Law Rev. **101**, 1079 (2013)
9. Ottis, R., Lorents, P.: Cyberspace: definition and implications. In: International Conference on Information Warfare and Security, p. 267. Academic Conferences International Limited, April 2010
10. Arquilla, J., Ronfeldt, D.: Cyberwar is coming! Comp. Strategy **12**(2), 141–165 (1993)

11. Parks, R.C., Duggan, D.P.: Principles of cyberwarfare. IEEE Secur. Priv. Mag. **9**(5), 30–35 (2011)

12. Wang, H., Wang, S.: Cyber warfare: steganography vs. steganalysis. Commun. ACM **47**(10), 76–82 (2004)

13. Catuogno, L., De Santis, A.: An internet role-game for the laboratory of network security course. In: ACM SIGCSE Bulletin, vol. 40, No. 3, pp. 240–244. ACM, June 2008

14. Rid, T.: Cyber war will not take place. J. Strateg. Stud. **35**(1), 5–32 (2012)

15. Nicholson, A., Webber, S., Dyer, S., Patel, T., Janicke, H.: SCADA security in the light of Cyber-Warfare. Comput. Secur. **31**(4), 418–436 (2012)

16. Schaap, A.J.: Cyber warfare operations: development and use under international law. AFL Rev. **64**, 121 (2009)

17. Nye Jr., J.S.: Nuclear Lessons for Cyber Security. Air Univ. Press Maxwell, AFB, AL (2011)

18. Cimbala, S.J.: Nuclear crisis management and "Cyberwar" phishing for trouble. Strateg. Stud. Q. **5**(1), 117–131 (2011)

19. Liles, S., Dietz, J.E., Rogers, M., Larson, D.: Applying traditional military principles to cyber warfare. In: 2012 4th International Conference on Cyber Conflict (CYCON 2012), June 2012

20. Reich, P.C., Weinstein, S., Wild, C., Cabanlong, A.S.: Cyber warfare: a review of theories, law, policies, actual incidents–and the dilemma of anonymity. Eur. J. Law Technol. **1**(2), 1–58 (2010)

21. Arquilla, J.: Computer Mouse That Roared: Cyberwar in the Twenty-First Century. Brown J. World Aff. **18**, 39 (2011)

22. Alford, L.D.: Cyber warfare: Protecting military systems. AIR FORCE MATERIEL COMMAND WRIGHT-PATTERSON AFB OH (2000)

23. Cahill, T.P., Rozinov, K., Mule, C.: Cyber warfare peacekeeping. In: Information Assurance Workshop, 2003. IEEE Systems, Man and Cybernetics Society, pp. 100–106. IEEE, June 2003

24. Taddeo, M.: An analysis for a just cyber warfare. In: 2012 4th International Conference on Cyber Conflict (CYCON 2012), pp. 1–10. IEEE, June 2012

25. Ganji, M., Dehghantanha, A., IzuraUdzir, N., Damshenas, M.: Cyber warfare trends and future. Adv. Inform. Sci. Serv. Sci. **5**(13), 1 (2013)

26. Leblanc, S.P., Partington, A., Chapman, I., Bernier, M.: An overview of cyber attack and computer network operations simulation. In: Proceedings of the 2011 Military Modeling & Simulation Symposium, pp. 92–100. Society for Computer Simulation International, April 2011

27. Chappelle, W., McDonald, K., Christensen, J., Prince, L., Goodman, T., Thompson, W., Hayes, W.: Sources of Occupational Stress and Prevalence of Burnout and Clinical Distress Among US Air Force Cyber Warfare Operators (No. AFRL-SA-WP-TR-2013-0006). SCHOOL OF AEROSPACE MEDICINE WRIGHT PATTERSON AFB OH (2013)

28. Kirsch, C.M.: Science fiction no more: cyber Warfare and the United States. Denver J. Int. Law Policy **40**, 620 (2011)

29. Turns, D.: Cyber warfare and the notion of direct participation in hostilities. J. Conflict Secur. Law **17**(2), 279–297 (2012)

30. DoD, U. S. JP1-02: Department of Defense Dictionary of Military and Associated Terms. Washington: DoD (2010)

31. Uma, M., Padmavathi, G.: A survey on various cyber attacks and their classification. Int. J. Netw. Secur. **15**(5), 390–396 (2013)

32. Saad, S., Bazan, S., Varin, C.: Asymmetric Cyber-warfare between Israel and Hezbollah: the Web as a new strategic battlefield. In: Proceedings of the ACM WebSci 2011, Koblenz, Germany, 14–17 June 2011 (2011)

33. Caplan, N.: Cyber war: the challenge to national security. Glob. Secur. Stud. **4**(1), 93–115 (2013)

34. Feil, J.A.: Cyberwar and unmanned aerial vehicles: using new technologies, from espionage to action. Case West. Reserve J. Int. Law **45**, 513 (2012)
35. Jolley, J.D.: Article 2 (4) and Cyber Warfare: How do Old Rules Control the Brave New World?. Available at SSRN 2128301 (2012)
36. Clarke, R.A., Knake, R.K.: Cyber war. HarperCollins (2011)
37. Gervais, M.: Cyber Attacks and the Laws of War. Berkeley J. Int. Law **30**(2) (2011)
38. McGraw, G.: Cyber war is inevitable (unless we build security in). J. Strateg. Stud. **36**(1), 109–119 (2013)
39. Robinson, M., Jones, K., Janicke, H.: Cyber warfare: Issues and challenges. Comput. Secur. **49**, 70–94 (2015)
40. Lindsay, J.R.: Stuxnet and the limits of cyber warfare. Secur. Stud. **22**(3), 365–404 (2013)
41. Junio, T.J.: How probable is cyber war? Bringing IR theory back in to the cyber conflict debate. J. Strateg. Stud. **36**(1), 125–133 (2013)
42. Liff, A.P.: The proliferation of cyberwarfare capabilities and interstate war, redux: liff responds to junio. J. Strateg. Stud. **36**(1), 134–138 (2013)
43. Erbacher, R.F.: Extending command and control infrastructures to cyber warfare assets. In: 2005 IEEE International Conference on Systems, Man and Cybernetics, vol. 4, pp. 3331–3337. IEEE, October 2005
44. Birdwell, M.B., Mills, R.: War fighting in cyberspace: evolving force presentation and command and control. AIR UNIV MAXWELL AFB AL AIR FORCE RESEARCH INST (2011)
45. Libicki, M.C.: Cyberwar as a confidence game. Strateg. Stud. Q. **5** (2011)
46. Brenner, S.W., Clarke, L.L.: Civilians in cyberwarfare: conscripts. Vand. J. Trans. Law **43**, 1011 (2010)
47. Swanson, L.: Era of cyber warfare: applying international humanitarian law to the 2008 Russian-Georgian Cyber Conflict. Loyola Los Angeles Int. Comp. Law Rev. **32**, 303 (2010)
48. Scott, A., Hardy, T.J., Martin, R.K., Thomas, R.W.: What are the roles of electronic and cyber warfare in cognitive radio security? In: 2011 IEEE 54th International Midwest Symposium on Circuits and Systems (MWSCAS), pp. 1–4. IEEE, August 2011
49. Roberts, S.: Cyber wars: applying conventional laws to war to cyber warfare and non-state actors. Northern Ky Law Rev. **41**, 535 (2014)
50. Dipert, R.R.: Other-than-Internet (OTI) cyberwarfare: challenges for ethics, law, and policy. J. Mil. Ethics **12**(1), 34–53 (2013)
51. Golling, M., Stelte, B.: Requirements for a future EWS-Cyber Defence in the internet of the future. In: 2011 3rd International Conference on Cyber Conflict, pp. 1–16. IEEE, June 2011
52. Bachmann, S.D.O.V.: Hybrid threats, cyber warfare and NATO's comprehensive approach for countering 21st century threats–mapping the new frontier of global risk and security management. Amicus Curiae, 88 (2012)
53. Danks, D., Danks, J.H.: The moral permissibility of automated responses during cyberwarfare. J. Mil. Ethics **12**(1), 18–33 (2013)
54. Friesen, T.L.: Resolving tomorrow's conflicts today: how new developments within the UN security council can be used to combat cyberwarfare. Naval Law Rev. **58**, 89 (2009)
55. Hunker, J.: Cyber war and cyber power. Issues for NATO doctrine (2010)
56. Hughes, R.: A treaty for cyberspace. Int. Aff. **86**(2), 523–541 (2010)
57. Solis, G.D.: Cyber warfare. Mil. Law Rev. **219**, 1 (2014)
58. Eom, J.H., Kim, N.U., Kim, S.H., Chung, T.M.: Cyber military strategy for cyberspace superiority in cyber warfare. In: 2012 International Conference on Cyber Security, Cyber Warfare and Digital Forensic (CyberSec), pp. 295–299. IEEE, June 2012
59. Dycus, S.: Congress's role in cyber warfare. J. Nat. Secur. Law Policy **4**, 153 (2010)

60. Clemmons, B.Q., Brown, G.D.: Cyberwarfare: ways, warriors and weapons of mass destruction. Mil. Rev. **79**(5), 35 (1999)
61. Lupovici, A.: Cyber warfare and deterrence: trends and challenges in research. Mil. Strateg. Aff. **3**(3), 49–62 (2011)
62. Stytz, M.R., Banks, S.B.: Addressing Simulation Issues Posed by Cyber Warfare Technologies. SCS M&S Magazine. n (3) (2010)
63. Libicki, M.C.: Why cyber war will not and should not have its grand strategist. AIR UNIV MAXWELL AFB AL AIR FORCE RESEARCH INST (2014)
64. Huntley, T.C.: Controlling the use of force in cyber space: the application of the law of armed conflict during a time of fundamental change in the nature of warfare. Naval Law Rev. **60**, 1 (2010)
65. Droege, C.: Get off my cloud: cyber warfare, international humanitarian law, and the protection of civilians. Int. Rev. Red Cross **94**(886), 533–578 (2012)
66. Von Clausewitz, C.: On war, vol. 1. N. Trübner & Company, London (1873)

Differentiating the Investigation Response Process of Cyber Security Incident for LEAs

Shou-Ching Hsiao[1] and Da-Yu Kao[2(✉)]

[1] New Taipei City Police Department, Haishan Precinct,
New Taipei City 220, Taiwan
[2] Department of Information Management,
Central Police University, Taoyuan City 333, Taiwan
camel@mail.cpu.edu.tw

Abstract. The number of cybercrime involving digital evidence will continue to increase as Internet become more intertwined in society. As criminals deny committing crime, Law Enforcement Agencies (LEAs) are hindered by the limited processing capabilities of human analysis. This paper presents a practical digital forensics framework of exploring ISO/IEC 27043: 2015 activities to lessen the caseload burden. It provides a suggestion for applying the Helix3 function to meet the need of incident investigation processes at scene or lab. While live investigative response at scene puts emphasis on finding actionable intelligence immediately, dead forensic analysis at lab pays great attention to reconstructing the case and conducting cross–examination to find the truth. Both are critical in the investigation response of cyber security incident.

Keywords: Digital forensics · ISO/IEC 27043: 2015 · Investigation response · Cyber security · Forensic analysis

1 Introduction

ISO/IEC 27043: 2015 offers a pragmatic approach for government agencies, private sectors, and international organizations [12]. Although it is based on idealized models for enterprise security incidents, Law Enforcement Agencies (LEAs) can apply such process on cybercrime investigations, differentiate the investigation response process of cyber security incident, and focus on the effect of people, process, and technology.

1.1 People: Governance on Digital Forensics

The dependence on using digital forensic tools or techniques brings about some potential risks, such as a framework for digital forensic science, the trustworthiness of digital evidence, detection and recovery of hidden data, network forensics. The challenges for LEAs are to ensure the integrity and validity of digital evidence [10]. The trend of digital forensics implies the imperative need for governance on digital forensics. They should persistently upgrade their skills, tools, and know-how to keep pace with changing technology. It is no longer able to simply unplug a computer and

© Springer International Publishing AG 2017
G.A. Wang et al. (Eds.): PAISI 2017, LNCS 10241, pp. 34–48, 2017.
DOI: 10.1007/978-3-319-57463-9_3

expand the backlog as a mountain at lab [20]. Investigators should know how to capture an image of the volatile evidence, use appropriate tools, and perform live investigative response.

1.2   Process: ISO/IEC 27043: 2015

LEAs expect to conduct an effective investigation, and create a corresponding increase of cybercrime conviction rate. The main impediment to pursuing these cybercrimes may be deficient in the suitable processes. The ISO/IEC 27043: 2015 international standards can provide some guidance of incident investigation processes when judges, attorneys, or jurors harbor doubts about the reliability and validity of digital evidence. In order to solve such plights, it is urgent to highlight a comprehensive process.

1.3   Technology: Helix3 Toolkits

There is an abundance of forensic tools on the Internet. Helix3 is a popular forensic tool, and has implemented numerous acquisition functions in cybercrime investigation [9]. Some LEAs have adopted Helix3 as their forensic acquisition method.

Literature reviews are presented in Sect. 2. Section 3 analyzes ISO/IEC 27043: 2015 process class and activity in cyber security incident for LEAs. In Sect. 4, the implementation framework on free Helix3 toolkits is explored to two phases: live investigative response in windows mode and dead forensic analysis in Linux/Ubuntu mode. Our conclusions are given in Sect. 5.

2   Reviews

There are two corresponding procedures for LEAs to exercise a good digital forensic practice. They are the live investigative response at the very first time at front crime scene, and dead forensic analysis at back-end lab [11]. From the aspect of live investigative response, investigators aim to implement the process of initialization and acquisition instantly after the case occurred. On the other hand, back-end forensic analysis at lab mainly deals with devices that has been collected or acquired at scene. By scrutinizing digital contents, the interpretation of digital evidence allows them to fully understand what actions has been performed and how the crime case is committed.

2.1   Crime Investigation and Forensic Science

The challenge of digital forensics lies in identifying important events in an efficient manner. The digital forensic process can be divided into the following two parts [6]: live investigative response at scene and dead forensic analysis at lab. Confusion on live investigative response or dead forensic analysis has motivated courts to explore some issues in the incident investigation processes of information security. Nowadays the drastically ubiquitous use of electronic devices in all spheres of life had contributed to the increasing demand on technology system [1]. Such devices include much criminal data and confidential information, and make it a top priority for LEAs to conduct an effective digital investigation. They face the challenges of analyzing and processing large amounts of data to determine criminal behaviors and cybercrime patterns [2].

2.1.1   Criminal Investigation at Scene

Criminal investigation should contain forensic science with modern scientific technique. Analyzing criminal methodology is necessary to identify suspects. The objective of criminal investigation is to clarify relation of people, matters, time, places and objects through confirming the criminal methodologies, motives and targets [4]. It focuses on the identification of victims, the interview of witness, and the fact recovery of criminal event [19].

2.1.2   Forensic Science at Lab

Forensic science focuses on the scientific method to collect evidence by repetitive and verified way. Conclusion is the result of deduction from facts, and is the objective description. Comment or opinion is the conclusion based on scientific knowledge, test result or self-experience and somewhat subjective compared with conclusion [4]. Investigators should always offer objective opinions and conclusions that are supported by facts. The conclusions, opinions, and recommendations should only be offered after a thorough analysis has been completed. Investigators should never offer an opinion or conclusion in court if they have not performed a proper examination of the evidence [21].

2.2   Traditional Digital Forensics

Digital forensics bridges computer science and judicial process. It is the fast growing field of science. Qualified investigators should make sure there is no destroyed, corrupted or changed evidence while they conduct forensic operation [4]. When evidence reliability is reviewed, trustworthiness of digital evidence should be verified in order to mitigate the errors at scene and lab. Traditional digital forensics only focuses on dead forensics, but the dynamic change status of digital evidence will be lost. That is the reason why LEAs should pay more attentions on live forensics or live investigative response.

2.2.1   Focus on Dead Forensics: Static Analysis of Image Evidence

There is an obstacle in the proposition of evidence collection by tradition forensics. Traditional forensic analysis is always operated by image analysis in order to mitigate the suspicion of altered evidence [19]. Forensic analysis will first try to recover the original state by forensic tools of Encase or FTK on the generated image file, but will eventually lose the information of volatile evidence, such as running programs, opening ports, and net status [17]. Digital evidence comes with dynamic features. Volatile attributes cannot be acquired due to limited time of complete image copy at scene. Chain of custody documents is created. It will result in accumulated cases at lab.

2.2.2   Loss on Live Forensics: Dynamic Change of Digital Evidence

The different records of digital data analysis always come after inconsistence of timestamp, initialization programs, execution procedure or computer state due to evidence dynamics [7]. To minimize this potential, LEAs must consider solutions to collect volatile data quickly and decisively. It is necessary to adopt live forensics of accessing evidence though it may somewhat change original evidence and system [8]. For instance, the digital evidence in cloud environment is dynamic and consisted of both data in local host and remote site. Evidence in local host is consisted of many evidence attributes in memory, temporary space, or files. Evidence from network environment is consisted of protocols, size of data packet, IP address of source and destination, port number of source and destination, and session time, which are not acquired by traditional forensics [7]. Most analysis in digital forensic science cannot make similar claims, and such evidence analysis should be interpreted for clarification. Failure to address live forensics will hurt the fact-finding activity.

3   Differentiating ISO/IEC 27043: 2015 Process Class and Activity in Cyber Security Incident for LEAs

This paper explores an overview analysis of ISO/IEC 27043: 2015 processes, and empowers LEAs to enforce digital forensic practices. Complying with the international standard, ISO/IEC 27043:2015, is an essential part for investigators to obtain the general credibility. Digital investigations comprise the following processes [12]: readiness, initialization, acquisitive, and investigative. Figure 1 consists of ten activities: plan, prepare, respond, identify, collect, acquire, preserve, understand, report, and close. These activities are iterative. Investigators can retrospect any processes even after that investigation process is done [15]. Lessons should be learnt to assist in the

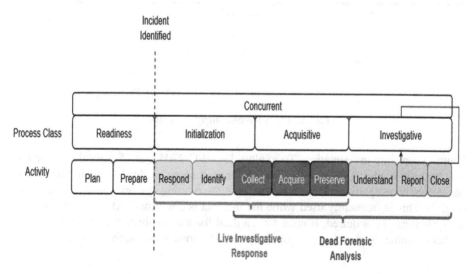

Fig. 1. ISO/IEC 27043: 2015 process class and activity in cyber security incident

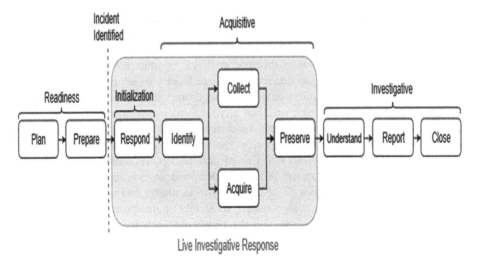

Fig. 2. Live investigative response at scene

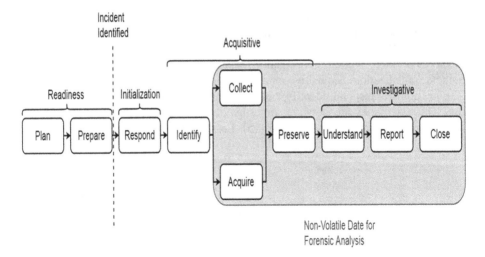

Fig. 3. Dead forensic analysis at lab

future cybercrime investigation. To explore ISO/IEC 27043: 2015 activities, there are two analysis modes: live investigative response at scene or dead forensic analysis at lab. A live investigative response occurs when the running system is analyzed at scene (Fig. 2). This is frequently used while the incident is confirmed. After it is confirmed, the system can be acquired. If necessary, a dead forensic analysis will be performed to further examine the data from a suspect system in a trusted environment at lab (Fig. 3).

3.1 Preparation

3.1.1 Readiness Processes

Investigators can take a proactive approach for preliminary planning in readiness processes, and form the digital forensic circuit before their forensic jobs. The potential digital evidence can be identified, collected, analyzed, or presented to meet the cybercrime investigation need of efficiency and effectiveness.

Plan

LEAs may suffer from poor planning when they face the ever-changing cybercrime. It is essential for them to verify their scope and purpose in an investigation [14]. A clear understanding of careful planning helps clarify the approach investigators take. The plan should work from general issues to specific requirements so that investigators can make right decision in identifying the criminal. It is critical to ensure that the following steps are implemented to present a proper report [13]:

- The investigation of cyber security incident is carried out in scientific method and in a professional manner.
- Some observations are proposed to describe an incident phenomenon. The formulation of a hypothesis is presented to explain the phenomena.
- The fact finding of forensic examinations may lead either to the confirmation of the hypothesis, or to the ruling out of the hypothesis.
- The incident investigation requires that a hypothesis be ruled out or modified if its predictions are clearly and repeatedly incompatible with digital evidences.
- Potential source of evidence are not overlooked.
- A systematic architecture is established.

Prepare

There are fundamental requirements for investigators, such as capable personnel training, standard operating process setting, forensic equipment preparing, file documenting, and so on. If servers are compromised, investigators should react quickly to carry out cybercrime investigation in a forensically sound manner.

3.2 Live Investigative Response for First Responders at Scene

When a computer system is power-on or online, its state is constantly changing. No matter what kind of toolkits investigators use on a live system, they will definitely influence the state of the computer system [19].

3.2.1 Initialization Processes

Once a cybercrime has occurred, the initialization processes trigger the commencement of the digital investigation, and concentrate on case management. This includes incident detection, first response, plan and preparation. A set of processes will lead well-trained individuals to implement an investigation. Initialization processes are compulsory in the corresponding forensic tools and detection techniques to tackle down cybercrime effectively.

Respond

The responding activity aims to scrutinize each crime case [16]. The time to respond to the case varies from the impact and genre. Since every computer system is vulnerable to hackers, responding to any cybercrime cases in a quick and efficient manner becomes top priority to mitigate the risk of threat from cybercrimes.

3.2.2 Acquisitive Processes

It is important to preserve the evidence, validate the ability of evidence, and prosecute the criminal. The acquisitive processes should incorporate the following activities: identification, collection, acquisition, and preservation. New challenges of cybercrime cases are presented to investigators due to the escalation need for live investigative response. Investigators may confront emergent circumstances such as running system that cannot be shut down, vast database server, encrypted file system, and volatile data getting lost [13]. Investigators should immediately consider utilizing Helix3 with well-built functionalities of forensic tools to access the device of their interest. To develop further insights into cybercrime cases, it is worth noticing not to compromise the evidence. Improper acquisition of digital device may cause the dismissal of evidence from court of law.

Identify

Forensic investigation cannot be fully realized without comprehensively identifying the potential evidence in cybercrime [4]. After appropriate and instant response to the cybercrime, investigators convert the acquired evidence to the readable form of identification activity. Correctly recognizing and determining the type and contents of the cybercrime cases will help the entire investigation to smoothly proceed. Once the type of cybercrime is ascertained, investigators can perform profile detection, network system monitoring, or cybercrime investigation in a systematic approach.

Collect

With the fast-growing numbers of cybercrime, investigators are increasingly facing situations in which the traditional forensic methodology of unplugging the power to a computer and then acquiring a bit-stream image of the system hard drive via a write blocker is no longer a viable option [20]. From the aspect of live investigative response to handling cybercrime cases, effective collection of digital evidence is quickly performed and is based on the life expectancy of that evidence in question. Backlogs are usually associated with cases waiting to be analyzed in crime labs. LEAs are struggling to reduce digital evidence backlogs in recent years. It becomes crucial for them to narrow down the cases, and keep high quality in handing every case. Live investigative response to conducting digital evidence has become a necessity.

Acquire

The shortfalls of traditional forensic method imply the essential need for development of live investigative response to acquiring digital evidence. Live investigative response remedies some problems from traditional forensic acquisition such as ineffectiveness against encryption and loss of volatile data [22]. It is essential for LEAs to collect the evidence immediately and prosecute criminals successfully after the detection of cybercrime activities. It means the evidence may inevitably be altered or modified, as long as investigators deem the situation appropriate to perform live collection on running systems. Helix3 may offer forensically sound methodology to seize the duplication of data and acquire valid digital evidence at scene or lab. To bolster the credibility and reliability of Helix3 toolkits, it is proper to fortify the admissibility of the acquired contents at scene by way of the video documentation during handling digital evidence or computing a checksum for the outcome of forensic tools.

Preserve

The evolution of myriads of cybercrime attacks has brought LEAs down face to face with the fact that traditional forensic analysis is no longer able to satisfy the requirements for preserving digital evidence [18]. Considerable effort in the forensic investigation is directed at guiding the first responder at cybercrime. Two main problems are respectively the vast amount of data storage and encrypted files. In live investigative response, the application of Helix3 proposes a solution to collect/analyze the running system without shutting down. It can preserve some valuable evidence with least modifications or obfuscation of the contents. As a general rule of thumb, investigators can ensure this kind of digital evidence as forensically sound and admissible one.

3.3   Dead Forensic Analysis for Lab Managers at Lab

3.3.1   Acquisitive Processes

Digital evidence remains uncontaminated and forensically useful in acquisitive processes [11]. These activities include potential digital evidence identification, collection, acquisition, transportation, and storage. The essence of acquisitive processes aims to sustain the evidence to combating cybercrime, and minimize impacts on the chain-of-custody integrity.

Collect

Actions or measures taken to collect digital evidence should be based on the approved methods and should not affect the integrity of that evidence [10]. For the sake of completeness of evidence, it is necessary for investigators to evaluate all evidence, prove the attacker's actions, and retain the incriminating evidence.

Acquire

This stage of activity starts when the potential digital evidence is collected and received by LEAs' forensic lab. Investigators should conduct a complete acquisition of digital devices, and determine whether they may contain potentially relevant data. Digital evidence can be easily altered, damaged, or destroyed. Improper handling or examination may be fatal to the integrity of the evidence [13].

Preserve

Due to the transient and fragile nature of digital evidence, failure to preserve the integrity may render it unusable or lead to inaccurate conclusion [19]. LEAs should understand the importance of their actions and consequences of accessing the original devices. They should take great care on the court admissibility of digital evidence. The careful documentation of digital evidence should comply with the chain of custody by chronological. They should implement appropriate protective and anti-contamination measures to keep the disturbance of digital evidence to the minimum. The collected digital device should be wrapped or secured in an appropriate container to avoid tampering or spoliation of the potential digital evidence that may reside in it [11].

3.3.2   Investigative Processes

Investigative processes involve processing a large amount of collected data forensically, achieving the goals of extracting evidence, and assessing relevant information [19]. In-depth file system analysis, such as analyzing the slack space, unallocated space in data layer and metadata layer, can be performed to reveal the content of hidden data and attain data recovery. Digital data pertinent to the incident must be collected and acquired in adequate manners. Any results from the assessment of extracted evidence need to draw a conclusion.

Understand

The understand activity aims to assess the obtained evidence quantitatively and qualitatively. The approaches to interpreting and analyzing digital evidence rely mostly on forensic tools. Capitalizing on these tools will improve the understanding, transparency, and readability for investigators. LEAs should be able to distinguish the difference between human-generated and computer-generated artifacts [21]. The efficiency and effectiveness of utilizing forensic tools are fundamental to reflect the contextual information in a cybercrime case.

Report

After a cybercrime investigation is complete, the investigator in LEAs may be invited to provide testimony in court. To deliver the finding in an investigation, a report should precisely describe its investigative processes, and introduce its technical methods to identify, collect, acquire, preserve, understand, and reconstruct the digital evidence [13]. The content of report should be written in a way that general audience can easily understand. Technological details should be translated adequately to non-technical people.

Close

The concepts of close activity review the results of the investigation. All evidence should be appropriately returned to the rightful owner or in a safe place.

4   A Proposed Framework of Exploring ISO/IEC 27043: 2015 Activities to Lessen the Caseload Burden for LEAs

As information technology advances, digital devices become portable and affordable. A series of methods dealing with digital evidence have been proposed to handle the investigation process for LEAs. Due to the customizable nature, Helix3 toolkits provide free attractive function to acquire evidence at scene or lab. It has been very difficult to integrate all of the information technology into the forensic science from live investigative response to the lab analysis. This proposed Helix3 framework expands from crime scene to forensic lab. Similar concepts can be applied to other software. Although each case is unique, a regular investigation framework always has something in common. In most circumstances, investigators can find key evidence during live investigative response, and put the case into an end. It becomes unnecessary to conduct a dead forensic analysis at scene for LEAs. By inspecting Helix forensic toolkits from the perspective of ISO/IEC 27043: 2015, the best practice for first responders and lab managers will be proposed respectively. It is designed to deal with the collection of live investigative response in Windows mode and the acquisition of dead forensic analysis in Linux mode.

4.1   Experiment Design

This experiment has set up a controlled environment to simulate the cybercrime issues.

4.1.1   Hardware

- ASUSTeK Computer Inc.

4.1.2   Software

- OS: Windows 8.1 Home Premium Version
- Forensic Tool: Helix3 (2009R1) (free download from http://www.e-fense.com/products.php)
- Virtual Machine: VMWare Workstation (10.0.3 build-1895310)

4.2   Toolkit Environment

Helix3 has developed a user-friendly interface in Windows mode to meet the need of live investigative response at scene. It helps gather information without losing potentially valuable information due to the system shutdown. Sometimes, servers and other critical resources cannot be turned off at scene. It can get an advanced insight into potential digital evidence, and assist investigators to judge whether or not the system contain valuable contents. Preserving the integrity of digital evidence is the basis for chain of custody in the process of investigations [3]. Since running live preview will inevitably interfere or modify the original data more or less, this acquisition method is only implemented for LEAs in exceptional situations or at scene so as to sustain the admissibility of evidence in the court.

4.2.1   Windows Mode at Scene

After investigators freely download the Windows mode of Helix3, mounting the "Helix2009R1" ISO file is the easiest way to explore it. During a live investigative response, a disk is loaded to the live machine and a virtual session is initiated with a set of toolkits to conduct live forensics.

4.2.2   Linux/Ubuntu Mode at Scene or Lab

Helix3 toolkits have an interface based on Linux/Ubuntu system, and are often installed in CD or USB for investigators to collect digital evidence at scene or lab. Investigators can set up their own customizable toolkits in USBs or CDs. To avoid leaving investigators' trail on the evidence system, it is suggested to boot them from a clean, forensic environment. Before booting up the target system, investigators should setup the BIOS to boot the system from the forensic USB or CD.

Live Investigative Response at Scene
For a live response, investigators can insert the Helix3 CD and use the function of Forensics & IR without any need for additional libraries or files. The following toolkits are included to reveal malicious activities, and respond to incidents quickly: Adepto, Autopsy, Bless Hex Editor, GtkHash, HFS Volume Browser, LinEn, Meld Diff Viewer, Ophcrack, Registry Viewer, Retriever, Virus Scanner, Wireshark, and Xfprot.

Dead Forensic Analysis at Lab
The dead forensic analysis refers to a static approach after investigators shut down the system. Helix3 toolkits are activated from the CD. The examined hard drives are mounted in read-only mode to impede evidence from contamination. Once Helix3 toolkits are switched to the Linux/Ubuntu mode, it becomes bootable and self-contained to focus on in-depth analysis of dead systems, such as keyword searching, integrity check, and hash image [9].

4.3   Analysis Mode of Exploring ISO/IEC 27043: 2015 Activities

4.3.1   Analysis Mode 1: Live Investigative Response at Scene

In ISO/IEC 27043: 2015, the live investigative response process ranges from initialization to acquisitive. At scene, there is no sufficient time for long-term acquisition or complicated analysis. The instant collection for volatile data is always the key to successful investigation [5]. By implementing those live responses activities, LEAs aim to efficiently and effectively identify the case and locate the essential evidence [15]. This section integrates Helix3 features to support the evidence collection. Multi-dimensional explorations in ISO/IEC 27043: 2015 activities for live investigative response are presented in Fig. 4 to comprise responding, identifying, collecting, acquiring, and preserving. These activities are illustrated in both sequential and procedural manner. The processes of live investigative response in Helix3 toolkits are further explored below.

Respond
Helix3 features include WFT (Windows Forensic Toolchest), FRU (First Responder Utility), File Recovery, Rootkit Revealer, Screen Capture, PC On/Off Time, Mozilla Cookie Viewer, USB Preview, and so on. It is useful for live investigative responders to immediately discover evidence, capture volatile forensic data, find actionable intelligence immediately, and get the evidence to the investigators much quicker [17].

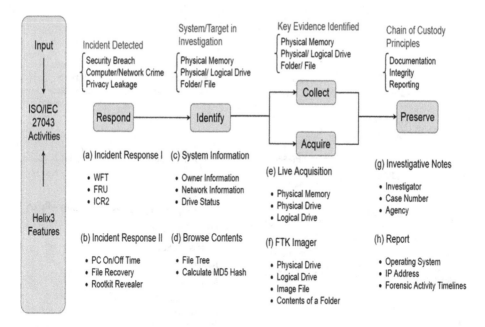

Fig. 4. Multi-dimensional explorations in ISO/IEC 27043: 2015 activities for live investigative response

Identify
First responders might be overwhelmed with the amount of information at scene. Investigators can respectively grab the system information and browse contents of target system, and immediately recognize where suspicious files or potential evidences locate.

Collect/Acquire
After identification, key evidence could be found from collecting or acquiring process. According to the order of volatility, collecting volatile data should always be privileged to preserve live memory, process, and network information. These would be lost in traditional forensic approach. Helix3 can support live acquisition on physical memory, physical drive or logical drive. It can start up FTK Imager for advanced acquisition.

Preserve
The chain of custody principles should always insert into preservation phase to ensure the integrity of evidence. The first responders can switch to Investigative Notes to fill up investigator name, case number and agency. Helix3 can automatically generate the report of whole processes.

4.3.2 Analysis Mode 2: Dead Forensic Analysis at Lab
After the live investigative response at scene, investigators will start conducting the dead forensic analysis at forensic lab. What forensic analysts find is always the smoking gun; therefore, analysis is the most complicated and important part in the

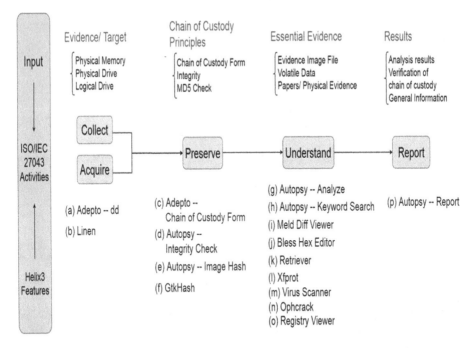

Fig. 5. Multi-dimensional explorations in ISO/IEC 27043: 2015 for dead forensic analysis

whole investigation. Figure 5 demonstrates multi-dimensional explorations in ISO/IEC 27043: 2015 for dead forensic analysis. The function of dead forensic analysis in Helix3 toolkits is also discussed and analyzed below.

Collect/Acquire

- Adepto: Let investigators select the destination and do hash verification.
- Linen: A Linux version of EnCase acquisition tool can select various imaging feature step by step.

Preserve

- Adepto: An in-built chain of custody form helps preserve the trace of investigation records.
- Autopsy: Produce hash value to validate the image, and ensure data integrity.
- GtkHash: Select a file and generate both MD5 and SHA1 hash value.

Understand

- Autopsy: There is a variety of analysis option.
- Autopsy: keyword searching helps investigators looking for essential trace or hex contents.

- Meld Diff Viewer: This tool allows investigators to see the changes in two files with a common ancestor. It can distinguish the difference between benign and contaminated files.
- Bless Hex Editor: Analyze a single file, and view the detail contents in several options.
- Retriever: Finding specific file types, such as graphics, word document, video, and so on.
- Xfprot: There are some scan options for this graphical malware detection toolkit.
- Virus Scanner: There are some scan options for this graphical virus detection toolkit in a digital forensic process.
- Ophcrack: In this Windows Password cracker software, investigators can update rainbow tables and import the password files to decrypt.
- Registry Viewer: Investigators can store registry file from Windows system, and analyze it in Registry Viewer.

Report

- Autopsy: Autopsy can create ASCII reports, and enable investigators to quickly make consistent data sheets during the investigation.

5 Conclusions

Cybercrime is a growing field in its diversity. Professional hackers can specialize in using various techniques. LEAs should be ready to plan and prepare their strategies to combat cybercrime. Any software has some limitations. Digital forensic solutions should not be limited in some commercial software. To combat cybercrime and put the criminals behind bars, investigators should take great care in handling digital devices. This paper increases awareness of ISO/IEC 27043:2015 processes within the digital forensic community, and shows how they can be utilized to solve lab backlog challenges. Investigators are able to apply Helix3 free toolkits to handle cybercrime cases, and fit in the international standard. It can produce a brief report of live investigative forensic and dead forensic analysis. This paper offers possibilities to conduct preliminary investigation at scene and in-depth analysis at lab effectively. Future research is needed to enable other software to support digital forensics.

Acknowledgment. This research was partially supported by the Ministry of Science and Technology of the Republic of China under the Grants MOST 105-2221-E-015-001.

References

1. Akhgar, B., Staniforth, A., Bosco, F.: Cyber Crime and Cyber Terrorism Investigator's Handbook, pp. 88–90. Elsevier Publishing, Amsterdam (2014)

2. Andress, J., Winterfeld, S., Ablon, L.: Cyber Warfare: Techniques, Tactics and Tools for Security Practitioners, 2nd edn., pp. 181–192. Elsevier Inc., Amsterdam (2014)
3. Bashir, M.S., Khan, M.N.A.: Triage in live digital forensic analysis. Int. J. Forensic Comput. Sci. (IJOFCS) 1(1), 35–44 (2013)
4. Brooks, C.L.: CHFI Computer Hacking Forensic Investigator Certification All-in-One Exam Guide, 1st edn., pp. 13–50. McGraw-Hill Education, New York (2015)
5. Cantrell, G.: Implementing the automated phases of the partially-automated digital triage process model. Digit. Forensics Secur. Law 7(4), 99–116 (2012)
6. Casey, E.: Handbook of Digital Forensics and Investigation, pp. 21–208. Elsevier Inc., Amsterdam (2010)
7. Casey, E.: Digital Evidence and Computer Crime: Forensic Science, Computers, and the Internet, 3rd edn., pp. 187–306. Elsevier Inc., Amsterdam (2011)
8. Casey, E.: Differentiating the phases of digital investigations. Digit. Invest. 19, A1–A3 (2016)
9. Official (ISC)²: CCFP-Certified Cyber Forensics Professional
10. E-fense. http://www.e-fense.com/. Accessed 16 Dec 2016
11. Graves, M.W.: Digital Archaeology: The Art and Science of Digital Forensics, pp. 91–110, Addison-Wesley, Boston (2014)
12. International Organization for Standardization (ISO): ISO/IEC 27037:2012 - Information Technology: Guidelines for Identification, Collection, Acquisition and Preservation of Digital Evidence. ISO Office (2012)
13. International Organization for Standardization (ISO): ISO/IEC 27043:2015 Information Technology - Security Techniques - Incident Investigation Principles and Processes. ISO Office (2015)
14. Johnson, L.: Computer Incident Response and Forensics Team Management: Conducting a Successful Incident Response, pp. 97–184. Elsevier Inc., Amsterdam (2013)
15. Ligh, M.H., Case, A., Levy, J., Walters, A.: The Art of Memory Forensics: Detecting Malware and Threats in Windows, Linux, and Mac Memory. Wiley Inc., Hoboken (2014)
16. Mrdovic, S., Huseinovic, A., Zajko, E.: Combining static and live digital forensic analysis in virtual environment. In: 2009 IEEE ICAT XXII International Symposium on Information, Communication and Automation Technologies, pp. 1–6 (2009)
17. Oriyano, S.P.: CEH v9: Certified Ethical Hacker Version 9 Study Guide, 3rd edn., pp. 1–222. Wiley Inc., Hoboken (2016)
18. Pearson, S., Watson, R.: Digital Triage Forensics: Processing the Digital Crime Scene. Elsevier Inc., Amsterdam (2010)
19. Richet, J.L: Cybersecurity Policies and Strategies for Cyberwarfare Prevention, pp. 62–204. IGI Global, Hershey (2015)
20. Roger, A.E., Achille, M.M.: Multi-perspective cybercrime investigation process modeling. Int. J. Appl. Inf. Syst. (IJAIS) 2(2), 14–20 (2012)
21. Scientific Working Group on Digital Evidence (SWGDE): SWGDE Best Practices for Computer Forensics, Version: 3.1, pp. 5–7. Scientific Working Group on Digital Evidence, Virginia (2014)
22. Stephenson, P.: Official (ISC)2® Guide to the Certified Cyber Forensics Professional (CCFP) Common Body of Knowledge (CBK), pp. 293–404. Auerbach Publications, Boca Raton (2014)

'Security Theater': On the Vulnerability of Classifiers to Exploratory Attacks

Tegjyot Singh Sethi[1]([✉]), Mehmed Kantardzic[1], and Joung Woo Ryu[2]

[1] Data Mining Lab, University of Louisville, Louisville, USA
{tegjyotsingh.sethi,mehmedkantardzic}@louisville.edu
[2] Onycom Inc., Seoul, Republic of Korea
ryu0914@gmail.com

Abstract. The increasing scale and sophistication of cyber-attacks has led to the adoption of machine learning based classification techniques, at the core of cybersecurity systems. These techniques promise scale and accuracy, which traditional rule/signature based methods cannot. However, classifiers operating in adversarial domains are vulnerable to evasion attacks by an adversary, who is capable of learning the behavior of the system by employing intelligently crafted probes. Classification accuracy in such domains provides a false sense of security, as detection can easily be evaded by carefully perturbing the input samples. In this paper, a generic data driven framework is presented, to analyze the vulnerability of classification systems to black box probing based attacks. The framework uses an *exploration-exploitation* based strategy, to understand an adversary's point of view of the attack-defense cycle. The adversary assumes a black box model of the defender's classifier and can launch indiscriminate attacks on it, without information of the defender's model type, training data or the domain of application. Experimental evaluation on 10 real world datasets demonstrates that even models having high perceived accuracy (>90%), by a defender, can be effectively circumvented with a high evasion rate (>95%, on average). The detailed attack algorithms, adversarial model and empirical evaluation, serve as a background for developing secure machine learning based systems.

Keywords: Adversary · Reverse engineering · Classification · Cybersecurity

1 Introduction

The Big Data revolution has fueled the development of scalable and practical machine learning systems, which has in turn led to their widespread adaptation and popularity. The domain of cybersecurity has also recognized the need for a data driven solution [1,2,4,6,27], owing to the increased scale and sophistication of attacks in recent times[1]. Although the use of machine learning techniques has

---

[1] https://www.statista.com/chart/2540/data-breaches/.

© Springer International Publishing AG 2017
G.A. Wang et al. (Eds.): PAISI 2017, LNCS 10241, pp. 49–63, 2017.
DOI: 10.1007/978-3-319-57463-9_4

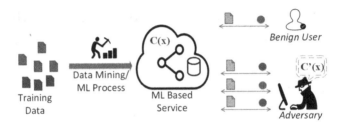

Fig. 1. Classifier systems in adversarial environments. An adversary making probes to the model $C(x)$ can use active learning to arrive at their own understanding of the model, as $C'(x)$. Probes are made through the same channels as by other users accessing the ML service, and as such can be indistinguishable.

found early success in many cybersecurity applications (such as spam filtering [11], CAPTCHA systems [10], and intrusion detection [6]), its own vulnerabilities have mostly been overlooked. Machine learning systems were designed under the assumption of stationarity, i.e. the training and the testing dataset should be identically and independently distributed [9]. This assumption is often violated in cybersecurity domains, as the systems operate in a dynamic and adversarial environment [1,4].

In an adversarial environment, the accuracy of classification has little significance if the deployed classifier can be easily evaded by an intelligent adversary [11]. Classifiers operating in such environments are susceptible to exploratory attacks by an adversary [1], who uses the same channel as the input data to probe the system inorder to gain information about it. As seen in Fig. 1, a model trained and deployed by a data miner (the *defender*) can provide services to end users, but it is also vulnerable to attacks, which use carefully crafted input samples to evade the classification. In doing so, the classifier system can be viewed as a black box (C), providing tacit *Accept/Reject* feedback [18]. This feedback can be harnessed by an adversary, who is also equipped with the knowledge of machine learning, to reverse engineer (C') the behavior of the black box and avoid detection on future samples. The symmetry of the attack-defense cycle and the new gamut of vulnerabilities introduced by using classification at the core of cybersecurity systems, warrants a data driven analysis of the problem and its effects.

The security of machine learning has garnered recent interest in literature [1,3,17,18,22,23]. A taxonomy of attacks against machine learning systems was proposed in [4], with Causative and Exploratory attacks being the broad classification of attacks, based on the portion of the data mining process they affect. Causative attacks affect the training data and are aimed at misleading the learned model. These attacks can poison the trained model, but can be prevented by careful curation of the training data [12] and by using data encryption techniques to safeguard the original training data. Exploratory attacks are more commonplace and dangerous, as they affect the testing phase data, which is often unlabeled and difficult to detect [2]. Using the same channels as a client user these attacks can masquerade as regular data samples, posing a risk to any deployed machine learning model. Mimicry attacks [22], spoofing [2] and reverse engineering [3] are all forms of exploratory attacks. Exploratory attacks cause the training and testing data distributions to drift, leading to non-stationarity and subsequent degradation in the predictive power of a classifier [11]. These attacks can affect any deployed system, even if the system is available only as a black box service. Recent advancements in black box *Machine-Learning-as a-Service* providers (such as Amazon AWS[2], Google Cloud Platform[3] and BigML[4]), promise a new era of flexibility and ubiquity in the usage of machine learning. However, preliminary analysis in [23] has shown that these services are vulnerable to exploratory attacks, by means of querying the system through their APIs. Membership inference attacks presented in [21], shows that these services are also vulnerable to data leakage, i.e. inferring whether a particular sample belongs to a model's training data, leading to privacy concerns in using machine learning models. The scope of these attacks can be made independent of the model trained and deployed as the black box. Deep neural networks were shown to be vulnerable in [17], who later extended their work in [18] to show how various classifiers, treated as transferable black boxes, are all equally vulnerable to such attacks.

This paper analyzes the vulnerability of classification systems to exploratory attacks, from a data driven perspective. The effects of an adversary, capable of accessing the system only as a black box; without any information about the learning process of the defender's classifier, is presented. To the best of our knowledge, this is the first work which aims at understanding attacks as a exploration-exploitation problem and presents data generation attack algorithms, using the classifier as a black box oracle. The following are the contributions of the proposed work:

- The vulnerabilities of classifiers operating in adversarial environments, to probing based attacks, is demonstrated. These attacks show that classification systems should not be naively used in cybersecurity applications, as they can be easily evaded.
- A domain independent and data-driven framework is presented, which can be used to simulate attacks on classifiers. Under this general framework, two specific attack algorithms are provided: the Anchor Points (AP) attacks and the Reverse Engineering (RE) attacks.
- Experimental analysis on 10 real world datasets demonstrate that only information about the feature space is sufficient to launch an attack against classifiers, while being agnostic of the type of classifier, the training dataset and the domain of application. This analysis serves as a background for developing secure machine learning frameworks.

The rest of the paper is organized as follows. Section 2 presents related work in the area of exploratory attacks on classifiers. Data driven attacks on binary

---

[2] https://aws.amazon.com/machine-learning/.

[3] https://cloud.google.com/prediction/.

[4] https://bigml.com/.

classifiers are presented in Sect. 3. Two specific strategies and algorithms are presented in Sects. 3.1 and 3.2, for generating simple probing attacks to complex reverse engineering attacks. Section 4 presents experimental evaluation on 10 real world datasets, 7 from classification domains and 3 from cybersecurity domains. Avenues for further development are presented in Sect. 5.

2   Related Work on Exploratory Attacks on Machine Learning Based Classifiers

Once a model is trained and deployed in a cybersecurity application, it is vulnerable to exploratory attacks. These attacks are non-intrusive and aim at gaining information about the system, which is then exploited to create evasive samples, to avoid detection. These attacks are universal and are difficult to eliminate by traditional encryption/security techniques, because they use the same access channels as regular client users and see the same black box view of the system. Work in [16], shows that linear and convex inducing classifier are all vulnerable to probing based exploratory attacks. Exploratory attacks are classified as either: *Targeted* or *Indiscriminate*, based on the specificity of the attacks [4]. Targeted attacks aim at modifying a specific set of malicious input samples, minimally, to disguise them as legitimate. Indiscriminate attacks are more general in their goals, as they aim to produce any sample which will avoid detection by the defender's model. Most work on exploratory attacks are concentrated on the targeted case, considering it as a constrained form of indiscriminate attacks, with the goal of starting with a malicious sample and making minimal modifications to them to avoid detection [5,14].

Particular strategies developed for performing exploratory attacks vary based on the amount of information available to the adversary, with a broad classification presented in [3] as: (a) Evasion attacks and (b) Reverse Engineering attacks. Evasion attacks are used when limited information about the system is available, such as a few legitimate samples only. An example of evasion is seen in case of the 'Good Words' attacks on spam classifiers, where the word *SALE* is modified to *SA1E*, to avoid being flagged [15]. In [26], a general purpose domain independent evasion technique was developed. Genetic programming was used to generate variants of a set of malicious samples, as per a monotonically increasing fitness function describing success of evasion. This technique is attractive due to its generality, but its practically is limited by the lack of a graded fitness function and limited probing budgets. The gradient descent attacks of [5] provides an efficient heuristic approach to utilizing the information about the classifier model, to generate optimal modification for targeted evasion of a set of data samples. However, the attack strategy relies on knowing the exact model of the defender and cannot be effectively used when only a black box interface to the defender's classifier is presented.

Reverse engineering attacks on classifiers, provides avenues for large scale evasion, as it conveys important internal information about the importance of features to the classification task. Reverse engineering was employed in [14], where a signed witness test was used to identify if a particular feature has a positive or a negative impact on the prediction decision. Reverse engineering of a decision tree model was presented in [25]. In [26], genetic programming was used as a model independent reverse engineering tool, assuming that the training data is known. The idea of reverse engineering was linked to that of active learning in [3]. Here, the robustness of Support Vector Machines (SVM) classifiers, to reverse engineering, was tested using active learning techniques of random sampling, uncertainty sampling and selective sampling.

In the above described targeted-exploratory attacks, it is assumed that an adversary would give up if an attack is expensive (far from the original samples). These attacks do not consider the case of a determined adversary intending to launch an indiscriminate attack. These type of attacks have been largely ignored, with the only mention we found was in [28], where it is termed - the free range attack, as an adversary is free to move about in the data space. Analyzing performance of models under such attack scenarios is essential to understanding its vulnerabilities in a more general and real world situation, where all types of attacks are possible. Also, while most recent methodologies develop attacks as an experimental tool to test their safety mechanisms, there is very few works [18,21,23], which have attempted to study the attack generation process itself. Our proposed work analyzes the vulnerability of classifiers to *Indiscriminate-Exploratory* attacks, where only a black box model of the defender is available. A data driven framework is proposed, thereby highlighting the symmetry of the problem of attack and defense, to motivate a data driven solution.

3   Data Driven Attacks on Classifiers

Data driven attacks on classification systems are exploratory in nature. An adversary proceeds by making probes to the classifier, by means of generated input samples, which it presents to the system. The feedback, a simple accept/reject in most cases, can then be used to infer the nature of the trained model. The classifier is seen only as a black box, which can provide binary feedback on input samples, in the same way as it provides classification on regular benign input data (Fig. 1). As an example, a spam classification system will not provide any information other than its intended behavior of marking input emails as spam, based on its analysis. In this setting, the model of an adversary can be formalized as follows:

- **Knowledge**: Adversary is aware of the number, range and type of features used by the system. This can be approximated from publicly available case studies or by educated guessing. No information about classifier type and training data is known.
- **Goals**: Adversary intends to produce false negatives for the classification.
- **Resources**: The attacker has access to the system as a client user. It can submit probe samples and receive feedback, up to a budget B, without being detected.

Based on the above model of an adversary, the problem of generating exploratory attacks can be formalized. A binary classifier C, trained on a set of training data D, is deployed to classify input samples as *Legitimate* or *Malicious*. An adversary aims to generate samples D'_{Attack}, such that $C(D'_{Attack})$ has a high false negative rate. The adversary has at its disposal a budget $B_{Explore}$ of probing data $D'_{Explore}$, which it can use to learn about C and understand it as C'. This setting represents a natural scenario where attackers start with limited reconnaissance and then launch a dedicated campaign, based on the learned vulnerabilities. An adversary operating in this scenario can utilize an **Explore-Exploit** strategy, popular in search based optimization techniques [24], to best utilize the budget $B_{Explore}$ to produce $D'_{Explore}$. Two specific instantiations of this general idea are presented here as the Anchor Points (AP) attack and the Reverse Engineering (RE) attack.

3.1   The Anchor Points(AP) Attack

Anchor Points attacks start with an adversary gaining information about a set of samples classified as *Legitimate* by the classifier C, which it then uses as *Anchors* to launch new attack instances. These attacks are characteristic of an adversary who has a limited probing budget $B_{Explore}$ and who wishes to quickly exploit a new found vulnerability, as is common in the case of zero day exploits [7].

From a data driven perspective, the attacks begin by obtaining a set of seed *Legitimate* samples D'_{Seed}. As an example, the adversary could start with a set of legitimate emails obtained from its' own inbox, for a spam evasion task. The obtained seed samples are then used to trigger the exploration phase as described in Algorithm 1. The exploration phase intends to obtain a set of *Anchor Points*, which will serve as ground truth for representing the space of samples classified as *Legitimate*. This exploration is performed using a radius based incremental neighborhood search around the seed samples, guided by the feedback from the black box classifier C. Diversity of search is ensured by dynamically updating the neighborhood radius R_i in every iteration, as given by (Line 5). This equation causes the radius of exploration to increase in cases where the number of legitimate samples obtained are high, thereby balancing diversity of search with its accuracy. Samples are explored by searching for a random sample within the radius of exploration, as given by (Line 6). The final exploration dataset of *Anchor Points* - $D'_{Explore}$, is comprised of all the explored samples x_i such that $C(x_i)$ is *Legitimate*. This is depicted in Fig. 2, as the set of positive points which are obtained at the end of the exploration cycle.

The explored anchor points set $D'_{Explore}$, serves as the basis to launch a dedicated attack campaign. Algorithm 2 incorporates information learned in the exploration phase, to generate the attack samples while also imparting diversity to the attack set D'_{Attack}. Diversity is imparted by adding random perturbation to the samples (Line 4) and then generating a sample based on their convex combination (Line 6), as inspired by the Synthetic Minority Oversampling Technique(SMOTE) for imbalanced datasets [8]. Random perturbation is controlled by the input parameter $R_{Exploit}$, which is kept close to R_{min} (Algorithm 1), as

---

Algorithm 1. AP- Exploration Phase

Input : Seed Data D'_{Seed}, Defender black box C. *Parameters*: Exploration budget $B_{Explore}$, Exploration neighborhood- $[R_{min}, R_{max}]$

Output: Exploration data set $D'_{Explore}$

1 $D'_{Explore} \leftarrow D'_{Seed}$

2 count_ legitimate=0

3 **for** $i = 1 .. B_{Explore}$ **do**

4     $x_i \leftarrow$ Select random sample from $D'_{Explore}$

5     $R_i = (R_{max} - R_{min}) * (count\_legitimate/i) + R_{min}$

6     $\hat{x}_i \leftarrow Perturb(x_i , R_i)$ ▷ Perturbed sample

7   **if** $C.predict(\hat{x}_i)$ *is Legitimate* **then**

8        $D'_{Explore} \cup \hat{x}_i$

9   count_legitimate $++$

10 **Procedure** Perturb(sample, R_{Neigh})

11   return sample+=random(mean=0, std=R_{Neigh})

Algorithm 2. AP- Exploitation Phase

Input : Exploration data set $D'_{Explore}$, Number of attacks N_{Attack}, Radius of Exploitation $R_{Exploit}$

Output: Attacks set D'_{Attack}

1 $D'_{Attack} \leftarrow []$

2 **for** $i = 1 .. N_{Attack}$ **do**

3     $x_A, x_B \leftarrow$ Select random samples from $D'_{Explore}$

4     $\hat{x_A}, \hat{x_B} \leftarrow Perturb(x_A, R_{Exploit}), Perturb(x_B, R_{Exploit})$

5     $\lambda = random(0, 1)$ ▷ Random number in [0,1]

6     $attack\_sample_i \leftarrow \hat{x_A} * \lambda + (1 - \lambda) * \hat{x_B}$

7     $D'_{Attack} \cup attack\_sample_i$

8 **Procedure** Perturb(sample, $R_{Exploit}$)

9   return sample+=random(mean=0, std=$R_{Exploit}$)

---

no explicit feedback from the black box C, is available in this phase. The final set of attack samples D'_{Attack} is submitted as attack on the classifier C, shown as red samples in Fig. 2. An adversary aims to cause a high false negative rate for C, while at the same time have high diversity in its attacks. D'_{Attack} is kept much larger than $B_{Explore}$ to justify adversarial budget expenditure.

The performance of the Anchor Points attack depends on the diversity and accuracy of samples collected in the exploration phase. Larger coverage ensures flexibility in the attack phase. By the nature of these attacks, they could be thwarted by blacklists capable of approximate matching [20]. Nevertheless, these techniques are suited for adhoc swift exploits, to cause impact before a defender has time to respond.

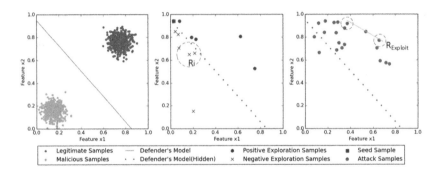

Fig. 2. Illustration of AP attacks on 2D synthetic data. *(Left - Right)*: The defender's model from training data. The Exploration phase depicting the seed (blue) and the anchor points samples. The Exploitation phase samples generated based on the anchor points, and submitted as attack payload. (Color figure online)

3.2 The Reverse Engineering(RE) Attack

These attacks aim to directly reverse engineer the classification boundary, so as to better understand the classification landscape, which can then be leveraged to launch large scale evasion attacks on the black box C. Reverse engineering could be a goal in itself, as it provides information about features importance to the classification task, or it could be a first step to launching an evasion or availability attack [3]. A reverse engineering attack, if done effectively, can avoid detection and can make retraining more difficult on the part of the defender. However, unlike the AP attack, the reverse engineering process is affected by the type of classifier model used by C, and is also dependent on the availability of sufficient exploration budget $B_{Explore}$, for the reverse engineering learning task. Nevertheless, an adversary motivated to evade the classification system is not concerned with fitting the decision boundary of C exactly. A linear approximation to the non linear defender's boundary is sufficient to launch a reduced accuracy attack, which can be compensated for by launching a massive attack campaign, utilizing the information provided by the reverse engineered model.

Effective reverse engineering depends on making best use of the $B_{Explore}$. Random sampling can lead to wasted probes, with no new information added. The query synthesis strategy of [24] generates samples close to the decision boundary and spreads these samples across the boundary, for better learning of the decision landscape. The approach in [24] was used for selecting samples for active learning. We modify the approach for the task of reverse engineering in Algorithm 3, where a surrogate classifier C' is learned as a result of the exploration phase. The algorithm begins by accepting a seed datasets, which is comprised of atleast one *Legitimate* and *Malicious* sample. The algorithm then employs the Gram-Schmidt process [24], to generate orthonormal samples near the midpoint of two randomly selected points of the opposite classes, as shown in Fig. 3. The magnitude of the orthonormal mid-perpendicular vector is set to λ_i, selected as random value in $[0,\lambda]$, to incorporate variability in the exploration

---

Algorithm 3. RE Exploration - Using Gram-Schmidt process.

Input : Seed Data D'_{Seed}, Defender black box model C. *Parameters*:
Exploration budget $B_{Explore}$, Magnitude of dispersion λ

Output: Exploration data Set $D'_{Explore}$, Surrogate classifier C'

1 $D'_{Explore\_L}$, $D'_{Explore\_M}$ = Legitimate, Malicious samples of D'_{Seed}
2 **for** $i = 1 .. B_{Explore}$ **do**
3   x_L, x_M ← Select random samples from $D'_{Explore\_L}$, $D'_{Explore\_M}$
4      $x_0 = x_L - x_M$
5   Generate random vector x_R
6      $x_R = x_R - \frac{<x_R, x_0>}{<x_0, x_0>} * x_0$ ▷ Gram-Schmidt process - x_R orthogonal to x_0
7      $\lambda_i = random(0, \lambda)$
8      $x_R = \frac{\lambda_i}{norm(x_R)} * x_R$ ▷ Set magnitude of orthogonal midperpendicular
9      $x_S = x_R + (x_L + x_M)/2$ ▷ Set x_R to midpoint
10   **if** $C.predict(x_S)$ is Legitimate **then**
11         $\lfloor$ $D'_{Explore\_L}$ ∪ x_S
12   **else**
13         $\lfloor$ $D'_{Explore\_M}$ ∪ x_S

14 $D'_{Explore} = D'_{Explore\_L}$ ∪ $D'_{Explore\_M}$
15 Train C' using $D'_{Explore}$ ▷ Training can be based on linear classifier of choice

---

phase (Line 8). The resulting exploration samples are then classified as Legitimate/Malicious by C, which can be probed upto $B_{Explore}$. The final combined dataset $D'_{Explore}$ (Line 14) is then used to train a linear classifier of choice, to form the surrogate reverse engineered model C' (Line 15).

The reverse engineered model C' can be used to crosscheck the randomly generated samples in the exploitation phase, to ensure that attacks have high accuracy. A practical and effective exploitation strategy is to use the $D'_{Explore}$ as the seed set for Algorithm 1, with the exception that we use C' to probe instead of the original C. Since the C' is a locally trained model, probing it does not impact $B_{Explore}$. Thereby allowing an adversary to make, theoretically, infinite queries to C', at effectively zero cost. The anchor points obtained can then be used to perform exploitation using Algorithm 2. The exploitation can use a large $R_{Exploit}$, as the results can be verified against the surrogate C', to ensure higher diversity and higher accuracy of attacks, than the AP attacks.

4   Empirical Evaluation

4.1   Experimental Setup

Experimental evaluation, presented here, shows an adversary's point of view of the classification system. The adversary is capable of generating data driven attacks on the system, by making limited probes to it and then generating a dedicated campaign of evasive samples. Since the adversary aims at evading the classification system, its efficacy is measured as the Effective Attack Rate(EAR),

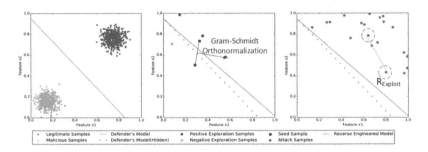

Fig. 3. Illustration of RE attacks on 2D synthetic data.*(Left - Right)*: The defender's model based on training data. The Exploration phase depicting reverse engineering using the Gram-Schmidt orthonormalization process. The Exploitation attack phase samples generated after validation from the surrogate classifier.

given by Eq. 1. This equation measures the accuracy of the attacks, from an adversary's point of view, and it indicates the false negative rate of the defender's classifier on the attack samples.

$$EAR = \frac{|\{x: \quad C(x) = Legitimate \quad \wedge \quad x \in D'_{Attack}\}|}{|D'_{Attack}|} \quad (1)$$

Here, C represents the defender's black box classifier and D'_{Attack} is the set of attack campaign samples generated by the adversary to attack C. The goal of an adversary is to maximize EAR.

The evaluation is performed using 10 binary classification datasets, shown in Table 1 (*Column 1*). The first 7 datasets represent standard classification tasks and were obtained from the UCI machine learning repository [13]. The Spambase dataset for email classification [13], the KDD99 intrusion detection dataset [13] and the CAPTCHA dataset for classifying human-bots based on behavioral data [10], represent 3 different cybersecurity applications which employ machine learning based classification at its core. All datasets were transformed to have numerical values normalized in the range of [0,1]. Instances were shuffled to remove any bias due to inherent concept drift. The class label 1 is taken as the *Malicious* class and 0 is taken as the *Legitimate* class, as convention.

In all experiments, the exploration probe budget $B_{Explore}$ is taken as 1000 and the number of attack samples to be generated N_{Attack} is taken as 2000. For the Anchor Points (AP) attack, the neighborhood radius $[R_{min}, R_{max}]$ is taken as [0.1,0.5] and the exploitation radius as $R_{Exploit} = 0.1$. In case of the reverse engineering (RE) attacks, a larger exploitation radius ($R_{Exploit}=0.5$) is considered, due to additional validation provided by the surrogate learned classifier C'. A SVM with linear kernel and high regularization constant (c=10) is taken for the surrogate classifier, to prevent overfitting to $D'_{Explore}$. The magnitude of dispersion (λ) is taken as 0.25, and it was found that changing this had little affect on the final results. In all experiments, no information about the black box C is known by the adversary. All experiments in this section are performed using

Table 1. Results of AP and RE attacks on a linear defender model on 10 real world datasets (EAR - Effective Attack Rate).

Dataset (#Instances, #Attributes)	Defender's initial accuracy	Explored anchor points/$B_{Explore}$	Accuracy of RE model C'	EAR	
				AP	RE
Digits08 (1500, 16)	0.98	0.63	0.92	0.96 ± 0.01	0.93 ± 0.06
Credit (1000, 61)	0.79	0.71	0.71	0.98 ± 0.01	0.8 ± 0.15
Cancer (699, 10)	0.97	0.99	0.95	0.99 ± 0.01	0.99 ± 0.01
Qsar (1055, 41)	0.87	0.99	0.42	0.99 ± 0.01	0.99 ± 0.01
Sonar (208, 60)	0.88	0.98	0.61	0.99 ± 0.01	0.98 ± 0.01
Theorem (3060, 51)	0.72	0.67	0.57	0.97 ± 0.01	0.87 ± 0.08
Diabetes (768, 8)	0.78	0.5	0.71	0.98 ± 0.01	0.95 ± 0.04
Spambase (4600, 57)	0.91	0.5	0.59	0.93 ± 0.01	0.71 ± 0.2
KDD99 (494021, 41)	0.99	0.91	0.55	0.99 ± 0.01	0.93 ± 0.04
CAPTCHA (1885, 26)	1.0	0.92	0.91	0.99 ± 0.01	0.97 ± 0.02

Python 2.7 and the scikit-learn library [19]. Results are averaged over 30 runs for every experiment. Section 4.2 presents the results of a symmetric case, where both the adversary and the defender have similar model types, while Sect. 4.3 presents analysis on non symmetric model types, with 4 different classifiers for the black box.

4.2   Experiments with Symmetric Defender Model

Experiments with a linear kernel SVM for the defender's model (regularization parameter, c = 1), is presented here, to show effects of a symmetric model type between the adversary and the defender. The initial accuracy of the defender, as perceived by cross-validation on its training dataset before deployment, is shown in Table 1. The Effective Attack Rate (EAR) shows that even models which are perceived to have a high accuracy (>70% in all 10 cases) by the defender, are effectively evaded by an adversary, with an EAR of 97.7% in case of the AP attacks and 91.2% for the RE attacks, on average. This shows the inherent vulnerability of the classification models and the misleading nature of accuracy, in an adversarial environment.

Both the attack methods of AP and RE are effective. The fundamental difference between the two approaches is that RE places its confidence in its understanding of the separating boundary, while the AP approach places its confidence only on the anchor points obtained during exploration. From Table 1, it is seen that the number of anchor points obtained is >50% of $B_{Explore}$ (*Column 3*), making it a simple attack strategy in high dimensional spaces. For the RE attack, the accuracy of the surrogate classifier C' (*Column 4*) is computed by evaluating it on the original dataset, as an adhoc metric of C's understanding of the original data space and the extent of reverse engineering. It is observed that even in

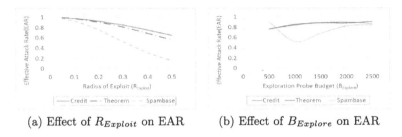

(a) Effect of $R_{Exploit}$ on EAR   (b) Effect of $B_{Explore}$ on EAR

Fig. 4. Improving diversity of attacks in AP leads to decreased EAR (a). In case of RE, which has high diversity, EAR can be improved by increasing $B_{Explore}$(b).

cases where the RE accuracy is low (0.41 for Qsar), a high EAR is seen (0.99). This is because, the goal of the adversary is not to totally reverse engineer the model C, but instead to learn it sufficiently enough to evade it. This enables the linear approximation technique of the RE approach to work as an effective attack strategy. The higher variability in EAR for the RE attacks is also a result of this approximation and its dependence on the quality of the exploration data.

While the AP attacks have a higher EAR than the RE attacks (Table 1), the RE approach provides better diversity of attacks, as it uses a larger $R_{Exploit} = 0.5$ (for AP,$R_{Exploit} = 0.1$). Diversity ensures that simple countermeasures of blacklisting will not thwart an attack [20]. The effect of increasing the $R_{Exploit}$ for the AP attack, in an attempt to increase its diversity, is shown in Fig. 4(a). It is seen that this leads to rapid deterioration in the EAR, as the only ground truth information available is the Anchor Points obtained during exploration. Increasing distance from these points leads to uncertainty and reduced accuracy of attacks. For the RE attacks, the datasets of - Cancer, Theorem and Spambase, are seen to have a low EAR in Table 1. Effects of increasing the $B_{Explore}$, in an attempt to increase the EAR is shown in Fig. 4(b). Increasing number of probes leads to an increase in the understanding of the black box C, which translates to better EAR. This increase plateaus after a critical mass of samples, needed for active learning the model C, is reached. This indicates the efficacy of the RE attacks as a long term attack strategy on a classification system, where over time the additional information learned can lead to both high accuracy and high diversity.

4.3   Experiments with Non-symmetric Defender Model

The development of the AP and the RE attack strategies considers a black box defender's model. These techniques are essentially data space search approaches, which are independent of the defender's underlying model type and their parameters. Results of testing the behavior of these attack strategies on a non-symmetric and non-linear defender models is presented in Table 2. The following defender black box models are considered: K-Nearest Neighbor classifier (KNN) with K = 3, SVM with a radial basis function kernel(SVM-RBF, $\gamma = 0.1$), C4.5 decision

Table 2. Effective Attack Rate (EAR) of AP and RE attacks, with non linear defender's model (Low EAR values are italicized.)

Dataset	KNN		SVM-RBF		DT		RF	
	AP	RE	AP	RE	AP	RE	AP	RE
Digits08	0.89	0.96	0.97	0.89	0.87	0.63	0.85	*0.48*
Credit	0.96	0.78	0.94	0.53	0.79	*0.42*	0.79	*0.33*
Cancer	0.99	0.99	0.99	0.99	0.97	0.89	0.99	0.98
Qsar	1	0.99	0.99	0.99	0.96	0.76	0.99	0.99
Sonar	0.99	0.98	1	1	0.97	0.62	0.99	0.95
Theorem	0.97	0.813	0.95	0.5	0.95	0.79	0.62	0.78
Diabetes	0.99	0.935	0.99	0.9	0.83	0.63	0.88	0.61
Spambase	0.93	0.99	*0.48*	0.84	*0.08*	*0.11*	0.99	0.98
KDD99	0.99	0.93	1	0.99	0.89	0.54	0.92	*0.27*
CAPTCHA	0.99	0.92	0.99	0.92	0.97	0.83	0.93	0.89

trees (DT), and random forest of 50 decision models (RF) [19]. The parameters of the experiments are kept the same as in Sect. 4.2.

It is seen that the AP approach is minimally affected by the choice of the defender's model. The RE attacks are affected by the choice of the model, as seen in the case of the Credit and the Theorem datasets. These datasets were seen to have a low accuracy, when trained using a linear model (Table 1), indicating non linearity in their model space. In these cases, the linear approximation in the RE approach, is not sufficient to have a high EAR. However, in a majority of the cases it is seen that a >50% attack rate is still possible with just a linear SVM model used for reverse engineering. A high average attack rate, irrespective of the underlying classifier used, indicates vulnerability of classification to purely data driven attacks. An interesting observation warranting further investigation is the comparatively low EAR on the decision tree models, which could be indicative of their attack resistance and its inverse relation to model robustness.

5   Conclusion and Future Work

We present a general data driven framework for demonstrating the vulnerability of classification systems to exploratory attacks at test time. Under this framework, two specific attack algorithms were developed: The Anchor Points attack (AP) and the Reverse Engineering attacks (RE). The effectiveness of these attack algorithms on 10 real world datasets, demonstrates that adversarial attacks can be launched having only the knowledge of the feature space of the data, agnostic of the defender's classifier type, training data and the domain of application. The defender's perceived accuracy was shown to be of little importance, if the model can be easily evaded by such probing based attacks. This is especially relevant in cybersecurity application domains, where the primary purpose of the classifier is to provide security. In these domains, it is worth emphasizing that - higher accuracy in machine learning does not necessarily imply better security.

While the proposed work presents the adversary's point of view of the attack-defense cycle, its goal is to move towards a more secure paradigm of using classifiers in cybersecurity domains, by clearly understanding its vulnerabilities. Future work will include attack detection and effective relearning, in environments with adversarial activity.

References

1. Abramson, M.: Toward adversarial online learning and the science of deceptive machines. In: 2015 AAAI Fall Symposium Series (2015)
2. Akhtar, Z., et al.: Robustness of multi-modal biometric systems under realistic spoof attacks against all traits. In: BIOMS 2011, pp. 1–6. IEEE (2011)
3. Alabdulmohsin, I.M., et al.: Adding robustness to support vector machines against adversarial reverse engineering. In: Proceedings of the 23rd ACM International Conference on Information and Knowledge Management, pp. 231–240. ACM (2014)
4. Barreno, M., Nelson, B., Sears, R., Joseph, A.D., Tygar, J.D.: Can machine learning be secure? In: Proceedings of the 2006 ACM Symposium on Information, Computer and Communications Security, pp. 16–25. ACM (2006)
5. Biggio, B., Corona, I., Maiorca, D., Nelson, B., Šrndić, N., Laskov, P., Giacinto, G., Roli, F.: Evasion attacks against machine learning at test time. In: Blockeel, H., Kersting, K., Nijssen, S., Železný, F. (eds.) ECML PKDD 2013. LNCS (LNAI), vol. 8190, pp. 387–402. Springer, Heidelberg (2013). doi:10.1007/978-3-642-40994-3_25
6. Biggio, B., Fumera, G., Roli, F.: Security evaluation of pattern classifiers under attack. IEEE Trans. Knowl. Data Eng. **26**(4), 984–996 (2014)
7. Bilge, L., Dumitras, T.: Before we knew it: an empirical study of zero-day attacks in the real world. In: Proceedings of the 2012 ACM Conference on Computer and Communications Security, pp. 833–844. ACM (2012)
8. Chawla, N.V., et al.: SMOTE: synthetic minority over-sampling technique. J. Art. Intell. Res. **16**, 321–357 (2002)
9. Ditzler, G., Roveri, M., Alippi, C., Polikar, R.: Learning in nonstationary environments: a survey. IEEE Comput. Intell. Mag. **10**(4), 12–25 (2015)
10. D'Souza, D.F.: Avatar captcha: telling computers and humans apart via face classification and mouse dynamics. Electronic Theses and Dissertations-1715 (2014)
11. Kantchelian, A., et al.: Approaches to adversarial drift. In: Proceedings of the 2013 ACM Workshop on Artificial Intelligence and Security, pp. 99–110. ACM (2013)
12. Li, H., Chan, P.P.K.: An improved reject on negative impact defense. In: Wang, X., Pedrycz, W., Chan, P., He, Q. (eds.) ICMLC 2014. CCIS, vol. 481, pp. 452–459. Springer, Heidelberg (2014). doi:10.1007/978-3-662-45652-1_45
13. Lichman, M.: UCI machine learning repository (2013). http://archive.ics.uci.edu/ml
14. Lowd, D., Meek, C.: Adversarial learning. In: Proceedings of the Eleventh ACM SIGKDD International Conference on Knowledge Discovery in Data Mining, pp. 641–647. ACM (2005)
15. Lowd, D., Meek, C.: Good word attacks on statistical spam filters. In: CEAS (2005)
16. Nelson, B., Rubinstein, B.I., Huang, L., Joseph, A.D., Lau, S., Lee, S.J., Rao, S., Tran, A., Tygar, J.D.: Near-optimal evasion of convex-inducing classifiers. In: AISTATS, pp. 549–556 (2010)

17. Papernot, N., et al.: The limitations of deep learning in adversarial settings. In: IEEE European Symposium on Security and Privacy, pp. 372–387. IEEE (2016)
18. Papernot, N., McDaniel, P., Goodfellow, I.: Transferability in machine learning: from phenomena to black-box attacks using adversarial samples. arXiv preprint arXiv:1605.07277 (2016)
19. Pedregosa, F., et al.: Scikit-learn: machine learning in python. J. Mach. Learn. Res. 2825–2830 (2011)
20. Prakash, P., et al.: Phishnet: predictive blacklisting to detect phishing attacks. In: Proceedings of IEEE INFOCOM, pp. 1–5. IEEE (2010)
21. Shokri, R., Stronati, M., Shmatikov, V.: Membership inference attacks against machine learning models. arXiv preprint arXiv:1610.05820 (2016)
22. Smutz, C., Stavrou, A.: When a tree falls: using diversity in ensemble classifiers to identify evasion in malware detectors. In: NDSS Symposium (2016)
23. Tramèr, F., Zhang, F., Juels, A., Reiter, M.K., Ristenpart, T.: Stealing machine learning models via prediction APIs. arXiv preprint arXiv:1609.02943 (2016)
24. Wang, L., Hu, X., Yuan, B., Lu, J.: Active learning via query synthesis and nearest neighbour search. Neurocomputing **147**, 426–434 (2015)
25. Xu, L., Zhan, Z., Xu, S., Ye, K.: An evasion and counter-evasion study in malicious websites detection. In: 2014 IEEE Conference on Communications and Network Security (CNS), pp. 265–273. IEEE (2014)
26. Xu, W., Qi, Y., Evans, D.: Automatically evading classifiers. In: Proceedings of the 2016 Network and Distributed Systems Symposium (2016)
27. Zhou, Y., Kantarcioglu, M.: Modeling adversarial learning as nested stackelberg games. In: Bailey, J., Khan, L., Washio, T., Dobbie, G., Huang, J.Z., Wang, R. (eds.) PAKDD 2016. LNCS (LNAI), vol. 9652, pp. 350–362. Springer, Cham (2016). doi:10.1007/978-3-319-31750-2_28
28. Zhou, Y., Kantarcioglu, M., Thuraisingham, B., Xi, B.: Adversarial support vector machine learning. In: Proceedings of the 18th ACM SIGKDD International Conference on Knowledge Discovery and Data Mining, pp. 1059–1067. ACM (2012)

Network-Based Data Analytics

A Structural Based Community Similarity Algorithm and Its Application in Scientific Event Detection

Xiangfeng Meng, Yunhai Tong(✉), Xinhai Liu, Yiren Chen, and Shaohua Tan

Key Laboratory of Machine Perception, Center for Information Science,
Peking University, Beijing 100871, China
pku.ericmeng@foxmail.com, yhtong@pku.edu.cn

Abstract. Graph similarity has been a crucial topic in network science, and is widely used in network dynamics, graph monitoring and anomalous event detection. However, few studies have paid attention to community similarity. The fact that communities do not necessarily own sub-modularity structure determines that graph similarity algorithms can not be applied to communities directly. Besides, the existing graph similarity algorithms ignore the organization structure of networks. Two communities can be regarded as the same when both their vertices and structure are identical. Thus the existing algorithms are unable to detect anomalous events about the shift of communities' organization structure. In this paper, we propose a novel community similarity algorithm, which considers both the shift of vertices and the shift of communities' layered structure. The layered structure of communities categorizes nodes into different groups, depending on their influence in the community. Both the influence of each node and the shift of nodes' influence are expected to affect the similarity of two communities. Experiments on the synthetic data show that the novel algorithm performs better than the state-of-art algorithms. Besides, we apply the novel algorithm on the scientific data set, and identify meaningful anomalous events occurred in scientific mapping. The anomalous events are proved to correspond to the transition of topics for journal communities. It demonstrates that the novel algorithm is effective in detecting the anomalous events about the transition of communities' structure.

Keywords: Community similarity · Layered structure · k-shell · Anomalous event detection

1 Introduction

Community similarity is a crucial problem in various scenarios. It can be used to track the temporal communities [11], monitor the evolution of communities [8], track the changes over time, detect anomalies [10,14] and events [2] in temporal communities. Community similarity can also be used to study the behaviors of the social group [8].

© Springer International Publishing AG 2017
G.A. Wang et al. (Eds.): PAISI 2017, LNCS 10241, pp. 67–82, 2017.
DOI: 10.1007/978-3-319-57463-9_5

There have been researches on graph similarity and community tracking. Several algorithms have been proposed [1,12]. Though communities could be regarded as special networks, there is one major difference between communities and networks. Communities do not necessarily own sub-modularity structure, compared to networks and graphs. Thus some communities can not be divided into more fine-grained communities. The difference between networks and communities determines that graph similarity methods could not be used directly to calculate the similarity of communities.

Besides, the existing algorithms usually ignore the shift of communities' organization structure. Thus they fail to detect anomalous events about the shift of communities' organization structure. Intuitively, two communities could not be regarded as the same when their structure differs greatly, even if they share the same vertex set. For instance, the replacement of the leaders in a social group indicates that a subversion or a peaceful transition occurs in the group. It is expected that a convincing similarity algorithm should identify the shift of communities' structure.

This paper presents a novel algorithm to measure community similarity by considering the shift of communities' layered structure. The layered structure of communities categorizes nodes into different groups, such as groups of core nodes and groups of ordinary nodes, depending their influence. To measure both the shift of vertices and the shift of communities' structure, two weights are defined and assigned to each node. The first is the importance weight. It emphasizes that the influential nodes could affect the similarity of communities more greatly than that of ordinary nodes. The second is the persistence weight. It proposes that the shift of nodes' influence will weaken the similarity of two communities. By integrating these two weights, the novel algorithm is able to measure the shift of both vertices and community structure.

In addition, we apply the novel algorithm into the scholarly scientific data set. As proposed by scientific scientists, journal clusters are able to guide subject classification. Thus by tracking the changes in scientific data set, we try to reveal some anomalous events in scientific mapping.

The contributions of this paper are two-fold. First, we present a novel community similarity algorithm, which takes both the vertex overlapping and the shift of community structure into consideration. Therefore, it is able to detect anomalous events about the shift of structure in communities. Experiments on synthetic data set show that the novel algorithm outperforms the state-of-art algorithms. Second, we apply the novel algorithm on scientific data set, and identify some meaningful anomalous events in scientific mapping.

2   Related Works

2.1   Community Tracking

Community tracking is a fundamental step in community evolutionary analysis. Several community tracking strategies have been proposed. One widely used strategy is the overlapping of vertices in two communities. For two communities C_1 and C_2, the similarity between two communities is defined as:

$$sim = \frac{|V_1 \cap V_2|}{|V_1 \cup V_2|}, \tag{1}$$

where V_1 and V_2 stand for the vertex set of C_1 and C_2, respectively. Two communities are regarded as the same community when their similarity is beyond a certain threshold. Besides, Palla et al. [11] proposed that two communities from two adjacent periods are the same community, when these two communities are contained in a single community that is obtained by partitioning a joint network that integrates the two corresponding networks. These two strategies, however, ignore the shift of structure over time. Chen et al. [3] proposed a set of rules to decide the matching of communities, which is somewhat subjective, and strongly depends on expert's experience.

2.2 Graph Similarity

The problem of graph similarity are divided into two main categories [8]: (1) with known node correspondence; (2) with unknown node correspondence.

For the first category, various kinds of algorithms have been proposed. Papadimitriou et al. [12] propose 5 similarity measures for web graphs. Among them the best two strategies are the Signature Similarity and the Vertex/Edge Overlap similarity. Bunke [1] presents techniques used to track sudden changes in communications networks for performance monitoring. The best approaches are the Graph Edit Distance and Maximum Common Subgraph.

For the second category, previous studies have presented multiple algorithms. The most widely used algorithms include: λ-distance [1,13,15], which is based on the spectral method; algebraic connectivity method [5]; and algorithms based on various graph kernels [7].

There are two major differences between the existing graph similarity algorithms and the work in this paper. First, the existing algorithms usually ignore the shift of the layered structure of graphs. Second, communities do not necessarily own sub-modularity structure, compared to graphs and networks. So the existing algorithms could not be applied to communities directly. And a more specific method is required to measure community similarity.

2.3 Properties a Convincing Community Similarity Algorithm should Satisfy

Koutra et al. [8] presented a set of properties to measure the effectiveness of graph similarity algorithms. They proposed that a convincing algorithm should obey the identity property, the symmetric property and the zero property. Besides, the algorithms should also satisfy five other properties [8].

However, both these axioms and properties are proposed in terms of graphs and networks, which may not hold for communities. For instance, the edge importance emphasizes the edge changes that create disconnected components and punishes the changes with high penalty. As communities do not have to own evident sub-modularity structure, thus this property does not always hold. So a novel set of properties are required in community similarity algorithms.

3   Methodology

We present a novel structural based community similarity algorithm, aiming at solving the drawbacks suffered by the existing methods. The algorithm assumes that two communities should not be regarded as the same when their structure shifts greatly, even if they share the same set of vertices. Equivalently, the shift of communities' structure could be interpreted that an anomalous event occurs in that community.

In this section, we first present the basic idea of the novel community similarity algorithm. One crucial point in the novel algorithm is to measure the social influence of nodes in communities. Thus the k-shell decomposition method is adopted and briefly introduced. Then we present the novel community similarity algorithm. In addition, we also propose a set of properties that an effective community similarity algorithm should satisfy.

3.1   The Basic Idea of the Novel Community Similarity Algorithm

The novel algorithm assumes that community similarity is determined by both the shift of vertices and the shift of their structure. Intuitively, communities are organized with certain structure, such as the flat structure and the hierarchical structure. The structure categorizes nodes into different classes, which reflect the influence of nodes in the community. Thus the shift of communities' structure can be measured by the shift of all nodes' influence.

Intuitively, for one node u that belongs to two communities C_1 and C_2, the following properties should hold in an effective community similarity algorithm:

(1). If u is influential in both C_1 and C_2, it will strengthen the similarity of C_1 and C_2.
(2). If u is influential in one community, but ordinary in another community, it will weaken the similarity of C_1 and C_2.
(3). If u is ordinary in both communities, its influence on the community similarity is weak.

These properties show that community similarity is affected by two factors. The first one is the influence of nodes. Influential nodes are expected to be more crucial in community similarity measurement. Intuitively, when measuring the changes of one social group, the shift of group leaders should be emphasized. Thus the importance weight is defined to measure the influence of nodes in the community. The second is the shift of nodes' influence. The fact that any node is influential in one community but becomes ordinary in another will weaken the similarity of the two communities. Thus the persistence weight is defined to measure the shift of nodes' influence.

3.2   The Measurement of Nodes' Influence

Both the importance weight and the persistence weight depend on the influence of nodes in communities. Thus how to measure the influence of nodes in communities is crucial. This paper adopts the k-shell decomposition method [4] to measure the influence of nodes. As proposed by Lü [9], the k-shell decomposition method could identify the coreness of nodes, which is an effective indicator for nodes' influence power.

The k-shell decomposition method is carried out as follows. First one removes from the network all nodes with degree $k = 1$, and assigns the integer $ks = 1$ to them. This procedure is repeated iteratively until only nodes with degree $k \geq 2$ are left in the network. Subsequently, one removes all nodes with degree $k = 2$ and assigns the integer $ks = 2$ to them. Again, this procedure is repeated iteratively until only nodes with degree $k \geq 3$ are left in the network, and so on. This routine is applied until all nodes have been assigned to one of the k-shells.

Figure 1 shows an example of the community structure obtained by the k-shell decomposition method. In Fig. 1, nodes in this community are categorized into three classes. Nodes with $ks = 3$ are the most influential, and belong to the 'upper' class. These nodes are densely connected. Nodes with $ks = 1$ are the least influential, and belong to the 'lower' class. They usually locate at the periphery of the community. The rest nodes belong to the 'middle' class.

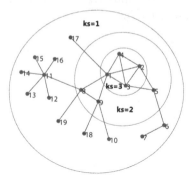

Fig. 1. The structure of a community obtained by the k-shell decomposition method

However, the k-shell decomposition method could only be applied to unweighted networks. To solve this problem, we adopt a derived k-shell decomposition method for weighted networks [6]. In detail, the weighted k-shell decomposition method applies the same pruning routine as the k-shell decomposition method [6], but is based on an alternative measure for node degree. This measurement considers both the degree of a node and the weights of its links, and assigns for each node a weighted degree, k'. The weighted degree of a node i is defined as:

$$k_i' = [k_i^\alpha (\sum_j^{k_i} w_{ij})^\beta]^{\frac{1}{\alpha+\beta}}, \tag{2}$$

where k_i stands for the degree of node i, and $\sum_j^{k_i} w_{ij}$ stands for the sum of node i's link weights. For simplicity, both α and β are set as 1, so that the weighted degree of a node i can be written as:

$$k_i' = \sqrt{k_i \sum_j^{k_i} w_{ij}}. \tag{3}$$

It is evident that when the weights of all edges are 1 in the networks, the weighted degree degenerates to the classical degree.

3.3   The Structural Based Community Similarity (SCS) Algorithm

We identify the influence of nodes by adopting the k-shell decomposition method, and present the definition of both the importance weight and the persistence weight here.

The Importance Weight of Nodes. We conduct the k-shell decomposition method in two large networks, and plot the distribution of nodes' k-shell values in Fig. 2. As shown in Fig. 2, in both networks, the number of nodes with certain k-shell value decreases exponentially as the k-shell value increases. Based on this fact, we assume that the importance weight of nodes should increase exponentially with their k-shell values.

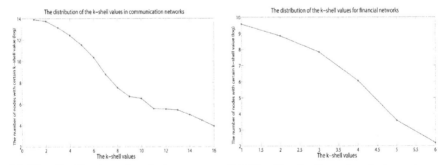

(a) The distribution of node importance in large communication networks (b) The distribution of node importance in large financial networks

Fig. 2. The distribution of node importance

Thus, given the influence of node i in both communities, which are denoted as k_{i_1} and k_{i_2}, the importance weight of node i is defined as:

$$weight\_i = 2^{(k_{i_1}+k_{i_2})/2-1}, \tag{4}$$

which indicates that one node owns high importance weight when it is influential in both two communities.

The Persistence Weight of Nodes. The persistence weight of nodes is defined as:

$$weight\_p = e^{-\tau*(k_{i_1}-k_{i_2})^2}, \tag{5}$$

where τ is the coefficient that determines the influence of the shift of nodes' status. Equation 5 shows that when the influence of one node remains unchanged in two communities, the persistence weight of the node is 1. Meanwhile, the persistence weight of one node will decrease greatly, when the influence of the node in two communities differs greatly.

Figures 3 and 4 show the distribution of the persistence weight with $\tau = 0.5$. In both two curves, k_1 and k_2 stand for the influence of nodes in two communities, respectively. In detail, Fig. 3 presents the distribution of the persistence weight with both k_1 and k_2 in the interval [0,10]. Figure 4 presents the distribution of the persistence weight with $k_2 = 2$. It can be seen that with the increase of the shift of nodes' influence, the persistence weight decreases sharply.

The Similarity Between Two Communities. For two communities C_1 and C_2, we denote that $O(C_1, C_2) = C_1 \cap C_2$ and that $F(C_1, C_2) = C_1 \cup C_2$. For each node i in the set $O(C_1, C_2)$, the influence of the node in the two communities are denoted as k_{i_1} and k_{i_2}, respectively. Thus the overall weight of node i is defined as:

$$2^{(k_{i_1}+k_{i_2})/2-1} * e^{-\tau*(k_{i_1}-k_{i_2})^2} \tag{6}$$

The overall similarity of two communities are defined as:

$$sim(C1, C2) = \frac{\sum_{i \in O(C1,C2)} 2^{(k_{i_1}+k_{i_2})/2-1} * e^{-\tau*(k_{i_1}-k_{i_1})^2}}{\sum_{i \in F(C1,C2)} 2^{(k_{i_1}+k_{i_1})/2-1}}, \tag{7}$$

where the denominator is a normalization formula, ensuring that the similarity of two communities is in the interval [0,1].

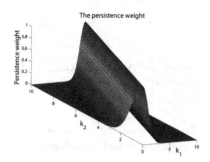

Fig. 3. The curve of the persistence weights

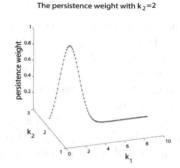

Fig. 4. The curve of the persistence weights when $k_2 = 2$

3.4 Properties a Convincing Community Similarity Algorithm should Satisfy

For two communities C_1 and C_2, the similarity between them should obey the following axioms [8]:

A1. Identity property: $sim(C_1, C_1) = 1$

A2. Symmetric property: $sim(C_1, C_2) = sim(C_2, C_1)$

A3. Zero property: $sim(C_1, C_2) \to 0$ for $n \to \infty$, when C_1 and C_2 are complementary in terms of edges or vertices.

Moreover, the measurement should also satisfy the following properties:

P1. [Edge importance]: Changes that lead to the shift of community structure should be penalized more than changes that maintain the layered structure of community.

P2. [Weight awareness]: In weighted graphs, the bigger the weight of the removed edge is, the greater the impact on the similarity measure should be.

P3. [Influence awareness]: Changes of nodes' influence with the same extension should be penalized equally.

4 Experiments

We apply the novel community similarity algorithm on both synthetic and real data set to test its effectiveness. First, we conduct experiments on small synthetic communities to test whether the novel algorithm obeys the proposed desired properties. Then we conduct the novel algorithm on the Web of Science data set, and try to identify anomalous events in scientific mapping.

4.1 Experiments on Synthetic Data Set

Experimental Setting. We conduct the experiments on small graphs as shown in Fig. 5, since people can argue about their similarities. These small graphs include cliques, stars, circles, and wheel-barbell graphs. Table 1 shows the name conventions for these small synthetic graphs. We compare our method to the 6 best state-of-the-art similarity algorithms:

1. Vertex Overlap [12] (VE)

The similarity between two graphs is defined as the ratio of nodes that exist in both graphs. It is usually used to track dynamic communities and analyze the community evolution.

2. Vertex/Edge Overlap [12] (VEO)

For two graphs $G_1 = (V_1, E_1)$ and $G_2 = (V_2, E_2)$, the similarity of these two graphs are measured by their vertex and edge overlapping, which is defined as:

$$sim_{VEO} = \frac{|V_1 \bigcap V_2| + |E_1 \bigcap E_2|}{|V_1 \bigcup V_2| + |E_1 \bigcup E_2|}. \tag{8}$$

3. DELTACON algorithm [8] (DA)

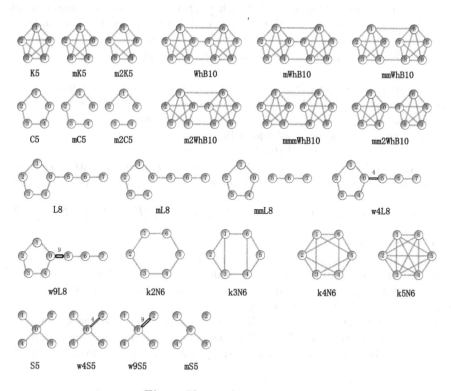

Fig. 5. The synthetic data set

Table 1. Name Conventions for small synthetic graphs. Missing number after the prefix implied $x = 1$.

Symbol	Meaning
K_n	Clique of size n
C_n	Cycle of size n
L_n	Lollipop of size n
S_n	Star of size n
WhB_n	Wheel barbell of size n
N_n	Ordinary network of size n
m_x	Missing X edges
mm_x	Missing X 'bridge' edges
w_x	Weight of edge
k_x	Graphs with nodes' k-shell values being k

It is proposed by Danai et al. [8], which is a principled, intuitive, and scalable algorithm that assesses the similarity between two graphs on the same nodes. It first obtains the pairwise node influence based on the random walks on networks, and then finds the similarity between the pairwise node influences in both two communities.

In detail, two versions of the DeltaCom algorithm are compared in this paper. The first one is the naive DeltaCon algorithm (DA1). And the second version is the scalable DeltaCon algorithm (DA2), which could deal with large scale networks. More details are available in [8].

4. Graph Edit Distance [1] (GED)

A simple GED algorithm considers the edit distance for both nodes and vertices. For two graphs $G_1 = (V_1, E_1)$ and $G_2 = (V_2, E_2)$, the GED is defined as:

$$ged(G_1, G_2) = |V_1| + |V_2| - 2|V_1 \cap V_2| + |E_1| + |E_2| - 2|E_1 \cap E_2|. \qquad (9)$$

5. Vertex ranking (VR)

Vertex ranking assumes that two graphs are similar if the rankings of their nodes are similar [12]. The vertices are usually ranked using their qualities, and the similarity of rankings is usually computed using a rank correlation method such as Spearman's rho (denoted ρ).

Given two graphs $G_1 = (V_1, E_1)$ and $G_2 = (V_2, E_2)$, for each graph we rank their vertices by using their influences, and obtain a sorted list of vertices. The ranking lists are denoted as π_1 and π_2. Thus the graph similarity can be defined as:

$$sim(G_1, G_2) = 1 - \frac{2 \sum_{v \in V_1 \cap V_2} w_v * (\pi_{1v} - \pi_{2v})^2}{D}, \qquad (10)$$

where π_{1v} and π_{2v} are the ranks of node v in both graphs, and D is a normalization factor that restraints the value of the fraction in the interval $[0,1]$.

6. The last 3 methods are variations of the well-studied spectral method 'λ-distance'.

Given $\{\lambda_{1i}\}_{i=1}^{V_1}$ and $\{\lambda_{2i}\}_{i=1}^{V_2}$ be the eigenvalues of the matrices that represent $G_1 = (V_1, E_1)$ and $G_2 = (V_2, E_2)$. Then, λ-distance is defined as:

$$d_\lambda(G_1, G_2) = \sqrt{\sum_{i=1}^{k}(\lambda_{1i} - \lambda_{2i})^2}, \qquad (11)$$

where $k = max\{|V_1|, |V_2|\}$. In case when the dimensions of $\{\lambda_{1i}\}_{i=1}^{V_1}$ and $\{\lambda_{2i}\}_{i=1}^{V_2}$ are different, a pad function should be defined which appends a number of values to the end of the shorter vector until the appropriate length is reached for the longer eigenvector. The variations of the method are based on three different matrix representations of the graphs: adjacency (λ-da), laplacian (λ-dl) and normalized laplacian matrix (λ-dn).

Experimental Results. The results for the three properties are presented in Tables 2, 3 and 4. For property P1, we compare the communities (A,B) and (A,C) and report the difference between the pairwise similarities/distances obtained by both the novel method and the 6 state-of-the-art methods. We've arranged the pairs of communities in such way that (A,B) are more similar than (A,C). Therefore, entries in Table 2 that are non-positive indicate that the corresponding method does not satisfy property P1. Similarly, for properties P2 and P3, we compare the communities (A,B) and (C,D) and report the difference in their pairwise similarity/distance scores.

Comparisons indicate that the novel algorithm is the only one that satisfy all the three properties. More detailed analysis is as follows.

P1. Edge Importance: Edges whose removal lead to great shifts of communities' layered structure are more important than those whose absence does not affect communities' layered structure. The more important an edge is, the more greatly it should affect the similarity or distance measurement.

For property P1, we adopt both the wheel barbell and lollipop communities. The idea is that edges that form the cores of the community are more important from the perspective of the layered structure, while edges that connect the ordinary nodes in one community are less important.

Table 2 shows the comparisons of these algorithms in terms of property P1. Two strategies are conducted in terms of the novel algorithm, with the value of τ being 0.5 and 1, respectively. It can be seen that only the novel algorithm succeeds in distinguishing the importance of the edges in terms of communities' layered structure, while all the other methods fail at least once.

P2. Weight Awareness: The absence of an edge with larger weight could weaken the similarity of two communities more greatly than that of an edge with smaller weights.

The weight of an edge defines the strength of the connection between two nodes, and can be viewed as a feature that relates to the importance of the edge in the graph. For property P2, we adopt the lollipop, star, path, cycle, and clique communities. The basic idea is that edges with larger weights play more crucial roles in community similarity.

Table 3 shows the comparisons of these algorithms in terms of property P2. It can be seen that four algorithms satisfy property P2, including our novel algorithm, the DeltaCon algorithm, the lambda distance in terms of both adjacent matrix and the laplacian matrix.

Table 2. Edge importance (P1): Highlighted entries violate P1.

Communities			SCS1	SCS2	VO	VEO	DA0	DA1	VR	GED	λ-da	λ-dl	λ-dn
A	B	C	$\Delta s = sim(A,B) - sim(A,C)$							$\Delta d = dist(A,C) - dist(A,B)$			
L8	mmL8	mL8	0.28	0.44	0	0	-0.01	-0.02	0	0	0.09	-0.12	0.08
WhB10	mmWhB10	mWhB10	0.16	0.26	0	0	-0.02	-0.01	0	0	-0.35	0.42	-0.03
WhB10	mmmWhB10	m2WhB10	0.12	0.37	0	0	-0.02	-0.01	0	0	0.12	0.23	0.06
WhB10	mm2WhB10	m2WhB10	0.39	0.63	0	0	-0.05	-0.03	0	0	-0.63	0.02	-0.08

Table 3. Weight awareness (P2): Highlighted entries violate P2.

Communities				SCS1	SCS2	VO	VEO	DA0	DA1	VR	GED	λ-da	λ-dl	λ-dn
A	B	C	D	$\Delta s = sim(A,B) - sim(C,D)$							$\Delta d = dist(C,D) - dist(A,B)$			
L8	w4L8	L8	w9L8	0.15	0.19	0	0	0.19	0.16	0	0	6.77	9.85	0.09
w4L8	mmL8	w9L8	mmL8	0.15	0.19	0	0	0.11	0.10	0	0	6.74	9.80	0.07
S5	w4S5	S5	w9S5	0.03	0.05	0	0	0.19	0.16	0	0	6.79	9.67	0
w4S5	mS5	w9S5	mS5	0.23	0.18	0	0	0.11	0.10	0	0	6.55	9.59	0
P5	w4P5	P5	w9P5	0.30	0.25	0	0	0.19	0.16	0	0	6.88	9.92	-0.02
w4P5	mP5	w9P5	mP5	0.23	0.18	0	0	0.11	0.10	0	0	6.88	9.87	-0.02
C5	w4C5	C5	w9C5	0.19	0.31	0	0	0.19	0.16	0	0	6.83	9.91	0.11
w4C5	mC5	w9C5	mC5	0.23	0.17	0	0	0.11	0.10	0	0	6.84	9.80	-0.11
K5	w4K5	K5	w25K5	0.19	0.31	0	0	0.52	0.43	0.3	0	24.70	45	-0.86
w4K5	mK5	w25K5	mK5	0.23	0.17	0	0	0.42	0.35	0.3	0	24.05	43.04	-1.41

P3: Influence Awareness: The density of connections in one community reflects how active the social group is. Thus the shift of communities' activeness should also be considered in the community similarity measurement. Changes of nodes' influence with the same extension should be penalized equally.

For this property, we consider a set of communities with different connection density. The connections in these 4 communities are densifying gradually, with their nodes' influence shifting from $k = 2$ to $k = 5$, respectively. It is expected that the similarity of any pair of communities with their nodes' status differing by a fixed value should be the same. Furthermore, the less one community's nodes' status shifts, the larger the similarity will be.

Table 4 presents the results for property P3. Different from the former two properties, the similarity of (A,B) is equivalent to the similarity of (C,D) for the first two rows in Table 4. Thus table entries with non-zero values mean that the corresponding method does not satisfy the property. It can be seen that only our novel algorithm satisfies property P3 for any case.

4.2   Experiments on Scholarly Data Set

The Scientific Data Set. We apply the novel algorithm on the scientific data set from Thomoson Rueters. It contains tens of millions of papers, academic reports and comments, from 1992 to 2011. We classify these data sets into four distinct periods, with each five years forming a single period. We obtain the

Table 4. Status awareness (P3): Highlighted entries violate P3.

Communities				SCS1	SCS2	VO	VEO	DA0	DA1	VR	GED	λ-da	λ-dl	λ-dn
A	B	C	D	$\Delta s = sim(A,B) - sim(C,D)$							$\Delta d = dist(C,D) - dist(A,B)$			
k2N6	k3N6	k3N6	k4N6	0	0	0	0.08	0.02	0.03	0	2	0.72	1.55	0.06
k2N6	k3N6	k4N6	k5N6	0	0	0	-0.04	-0.01	10^{-3}	0	0	1.05	1.01	-0.09
k2N6	k3N6	k2N6	k4N6	0.47	0.35	0	0.19	0.05	0.06	0	4	1.43	3.21	0.37
k2N6	k3N6	k2N6	k5N6	0.59	0.37	0	0.26	0.09	0.10	0	6	2.85	6.04	0.71

citation relations among journals by aggregating the citations from the level of papers. Two criteria are applied to select journals: at first, only the journals with at least 50 publications are investigated, and others are removed from the data set; then only those journals with more than 30 citations are kept. Thus four journal networks are formed, with nodes representing journals and edges representing the citation relations among journals. We adopt the spectral clustering algorithm to partition each journal network, and obtain 60 communities for each snapshot of the journal networks.

Experimental Results. We conduct both the vertex overlapping strategy and the novel algorithm to calculate the similarities of communities from adjacent periods. The comparison of the two strategies are plotted in Fig. 6. In Fig. 6, the x-axis stands for the similarity of communities obtained by the vertex overlapping strategy, the y-axis stands for the similarity of communities obtained by our novel algorithm, and the red line stands for the plot $y = x$.

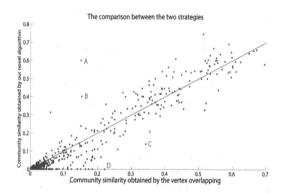

Fig. 6. Comparison of similarities measured by the two methods

It can be seen that for most pairs of communities, the two similarity values are located around the plot $y = x$. This indicates that the structure of the majority of journal communities remain stable over time. However, there are exceptions. Four cases are listed, as their similarities obtained by the vertex overlapping strategy and our novel algorithm differ greatly. Both the visualizations and the text annotations of communities in these four cases are presented.

For both cases of 'A' and 'B', the structural similarities obtained by the novel algorithm are much larger than that obtained by the vertex overlapping strategy. It indicates that the vertex sets in these communities shift greatly. Meanwhile, the structure of the community remains stable.

We visualize the pair of communities for case 'A' in Fig. 7. In Fig. 7, nodes with large sizes represent the core journals in communities. Though multiple journals are inserted in Fig. 7b, these new nodes lie mainly at the periphery of the community. And the core nodes in Fig. 7a remain influential in Fig. 7b.

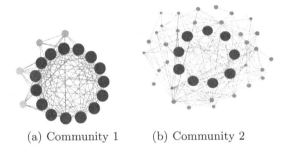

(a) Community 1   (b) Community 2

Fig. 7. The pair of communities for case A

Table 5. Text annotations of the four cases in Fig. 6

Cases	Comm	Text annotation
A	A1	Philology, classical, historical, roman
	A2	
B	B1	Biblical, catholic, jewish, fiction
	B2	
C	C1	Zoology, ecology, biology, evolutionary
	C2	Entomology, zoology, insect, invertebrate
D	D1	Information,library,documentation,electronic
	D2	Law, criminal, harvard, legal

Besides, we present the text annotations of the two communities in Table 5. It can be seen that the text annotations of both communities in case 'A' are 'philology, classical, historical, roman'.

Similarly, for case 'B', though the majority of nodes have changed, the set of core nodes remain stable. Thus the similarity of the two communities based on the novel algorithm is larger than the classical vertex overlapping strategy. Specifically, both the two communities in case 'B' are about the 'biblical, catholic, jewish, fiction'.

For both cases of 'C' and 'D', the similarities obtained by the vertex overlapping are much larger than that obtained by the novel algorithm. It indicates that although the vertex set of the communities remain relatively stable, the internal structure of these communities shifts greatly. A potential topic transition may have occurred in these communities.

As shown in Fig. 6, the two communities in case 'C' share 35% of their vertices. However, the layered structure of these two communities differ greatly. As shown in Fig. 8, the core nodes shift from one set of vertices to another. Furthermore, according to Table 5, these two communities focus on different subdisciplines about zoology. The first community prefers researches about both the ecology and biology. Meanwhile, the second community prefers to researches about animals, such as entomology, insects, and invertebrate.

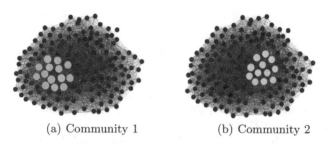

(a) Community 1   (b) Community 2

Fig. 8. The pair of communities for case C

Similarly, for case 'D', the first community prefers to the library and information science. However, the second community prefers to law and criminal researches. The difference of their topics demonstrate that the novel algorithm is effective to monitor the evolution of journal clusters.

5 Conclusions

This paper presents a novel similarity algorithm to measure the similarity of communities. It considers not only the overlapping of vertices, but also the shift of communities' structure over time. In the novel algorithm, two kinds of weights are defined and assigned to each node to measure the shift of community structure. The first is the importance weight, indicating that influential nodes play crucial roles in community similarity algorithms. The second is the persistence weight, indicating that the shift of nodes' influence will weaken the similarity of two communities, and vice versa. By considering the shift of communities' structure, the novel algorithm is able to detect anomalous events about the communities' structural transition.

Besides, we propose a set of desired properties a convincing community similarity algorithm should satisfy. We apply the novel algorithm on the synthetic data set, and demonstrate that the novel algorithm outperforms the state-of-art algorithms. In addition, we apply the novel algorithm in the scholarly data set, and identify some anomalous events that occur in scientific mapping. These identified events correspond to topic transitions in corresponding journal communities. The experiments indicate that the novel algorithm is effective to detect anomalous events about the shift of communities' internal structure.

The capacity of detecting communities' structural transition determines that the novel algorithm can be used to various sceneries, such as crime and fraud detection in social groups. In later studies, we will apply this algorithm to more sceneries, and further validate its effectiveness in anomalous event detection.

References

1. Bunke, H., Dickinson, P.J., Kraetzl, M., Wallis, W.D.: A Graph-theoretic Approach to Enterprise Network Dynamics, vol. 24. Springer Science & Business Media, New York (2007)
2. Caceres, R.S., Berger-Wolf, T., Grossman, R.: Temporal scale of processes in dynamic networks. In: 2011 IEEE 11th International Conference on Data Mining Workshops, pp. 925–932. IEEE (2011)
3. Chen, Z., Wilson, K.A., Jin, Y., Hendrix, W., Samatova, N.F.: Detecting and tracking community dynamics in evolutionary networks. In: 2010 IEEE International Conference on Data Mining Workshops, pp. 318–327. IEEE (2010)
4. Dorogovtsev, S.N., Goltsev, A.V., Mendes, J.F.F.: K-core organization of complex networks. Phys. Rev. Lett. **96**(4), 040601 (2006)
5. Fiedler, M.: Algebraic connectivity of graphs. Czech. Math. J. **23**(2), 298–305 (1973)
6. Garas, A., Schweitzer, F., Havlin, S.: A k-shell decomposition method for weighted networks. New J. Phys. **14**(8), 083030 (2012)
7. Kang, U., Tong, H., Sun, J.: Fast random walk graph kernel. In: SDM, pp. 828–838. SIAM (2012)
8. Koutra, D., Vogelstein, J.T., Faloutsos, C.: Deltacon: a principled massive-graph similarity function. In: Proceedings of the SIAM International Conference in Data Mining. Society for Industrial and Applied Mathematics, pp. 162–170. SIAM (2013)
9. Lü, L., Chen, D., Ren, X.-L., Zhang, Q.-M., Zhang, Y.-C., Zhou, T.: Vital nodes identification in complex networks. Phys. Rep. **650**, 1–63 (2016)
10. Noble, C.C., Cook, D.J.: Graph-based anomaly detection. In: Proceedings of the Ninth ACM SIGKDD International Conference on Knowledge Discovery and Data Mining, pp. 631–636. ACM (2003)
11. Palla, G., Barabási, A.-L., Vicsek, T.: Quantifying social group evolution. Nature **446**(7136), 664–667 (2007)
12. Papadimitriou, P., Dasdan, A., Garcia-Molina, H.: Web graph similarity for anomaly detection. J. Internet Serv. Appl. **1**(1), 19–30 (2010)
13. Peabody, M.: Finding groups of graphs in databases. Ph.D. thesis. Citeseer (2002)
14. Wang, Y., Parthasarathy, S., Tatikonda, S.: Locality sensitive outlier detection: a ranking driven approach. In: 2011 IEEE 27th International Conference on Data Engineering, pp. 410–421. IEEE (2011)
15. Wilson, R.C., Zhu, P.: A study of graph spectra for comparing graphs and trees. Pattern Recogn. **41**(9), 2833–2841 (2008)

Link Prediction in Temporal Heterogeneous Networks

T. Jaya Lakshmi[1,2(✉)] and S. Durga Bhavani[1]

[1] School of Computer and Information Sciences, University of Hyderabad,
Hyderabad, India
jaya.phd.hcu@gmail.com, sdbcs@uohyd.ernet.in
[2] Vasireddy Venkatadri Institute of Technology, Nambur, Andhra Pradesh, India

Abstract. Link prediction in temporal social networks addresses the problem of predicting future links. The problem of link prediction in heterogeneous networks is challenging due to the existence of multiple types of nodes and edges. There are many methods available in the literature for homogeneous networks, which rely on the network topology. In this work, we extend some of the standard measures viz Common Neighbors, Jaccard Coefficient, AdamicAdar, Time-score, Co-occurrence probabilistic measure and Temporal Co-occurrence probabilistic measure to heterogeneous networks. Probabilistic graphical models prove to be efficient for link prediction compared to topological methods. We incorporate the information related to time of link formation into probabilistic graphical models and generate a new measure called Heterogeneous Temporal Co-occurrence probability (*Hetero-TCOP*) measure for heterogeneous networks. We evaluate all the extended heterogeneous measures along with *Hetero-TCOP* on DBLP and HiePh bibliographic networks for predicting two types of links: author-conference/journal links and co-author links in the heterogeneous environment. In both cases, *Hetero-TCOP* achieves superior performance over the standard topological measures. In the case of DBLP dataset, *Hetero-TCOP* shows an improvement of 15% accuracy over neighborhood-based measures, 6% over temporal measures and 5% over Co-occurrence probability measure. Similar improvement in performance is observed for HeiPh dataset also.

1 Introduction

A social network modelled as a graph is called heterogeneous if it has multiple types of nodes and multiple type of edges. A multi-relational network contains single type of nodes and multiple types of edges. A bipartite network contains two types of nodes and an edge connects two vertices of different types.

Many networks in the real world are heterogeneous in nature. For instance, a bibliographic network may have multiple types of nodes such as author, paper, conference, venue and keywords. Two authors may be related with *co-authorship* relation; an author may *write* a paper; a paper may be *published* by a conference; an author *attends* a conference and a paper *contain* keywords. This scenario is depicted in Fig. 1.

© Springer International Publishing AG 2017
G.A. Wang et al. (Eds.): PAISI 2017, LNCS 10241, pp. 83–98, 2017.
DOI: 10.1007/978-3-319-57463-9_6

Fig. 1. DBLP heterogeneous network

We define a *homogeneous edge* as an edge between two nodes of same type and *heterogeneous edge* as an edge existing between nodes of different types. In Fig. 1, *co-authorship* edges are homogeneous and the *publish* edges between paper node and conference node are heterogeneous edges.

A social network is called as temporal network, if knowledge of formation-time of link is available [34]. **Link Prediction** is a task of predicting future links in temporal social networks and identifying missing links in non-temporal social network. Link prediction has many significant applications such as item recommendations in e-commerce sites, recommend friends in a friendship network, identify cross domain potential collaborators and infer links in partially observed network. In criminal networks, illicit interactions may be hidden and the information may not be available. The missing links in such cases may relate to the illegal intrusion of people with most probable co-participation. Link prediction can identify these hidden illicit activities in such networks [3,10,13].

The structure of heterogeneous network is more complex compared to homogeneous network because of existence of multiple types of nodes and edges. The relation between two nodes of same type may be influenced by the existence of multiple types of edges between them. So, solving link prediction problem using homogeneous projections does not yield good results.

Many link prediction measures in literature infer homogeneous links in social networks; recently more work is seen with reference to heterogeneous networks. In this paper, we extend the available link prediction measures to heterogeneous networks. In addition to that, a new probabilistic measure called Heterogeneous Temporal Co-occurrence probability (Hetero-TCOP) is proposed for bipartite and heterogeneous social networks. We evaluate the proposed measures on two collaborative datasets of DBLP and HiePh of *arXiv*. The proposed measures show an improvement in accuracy when heterogeneous information is included.

2   Literature Review

Mainly, there are two approaches for link prediction: proximity-based and machine learning-based [34].

Proximity-based approaches compute a score for pairs of unconnected nodes, and pairs with highest score are considered most likely to form in future. Common Neighbors, Jaccard Coefficient [20], Preferential Attachment, Adamic Adar [1], Katz [16], Rooted Page Rank, PropFlow [23] and Co-occurrence probability (COP) [32] are some of the popular proximity-based measures.

A machine learning-based approach models the link prediction problem as a binary classification task [13, 23]. The main challenge for machine learning approach for link prediction is the extreme class-skewness. The number of possible links is very high compared to the actual links present in the network, resulting in class skewness. Some techniques to handle imbalance are required. HPLP [23] uses undersampling [4] to handle class imbalance.

2.1   Link Prediction Literature for Heterogeneous Networks

A heterogeneous social network contains multiple types of nodes with homogeneous and heterogeneous edges existing between them. A multi-relational network contains multiple types of homogeneous edges between same type of nodes. A bipartite network contains two types of nodes and heterogeneous edges connecting the nodes while the homogeneous edges are suppressed. Davis et al. [7], Lichtenwalter et al. [22] and Han et al. [35] propose solutions for link prediction problem in multi-relational networks. Benchettara et al. [2] predict future links of a bipartite graph by constructing homogeneous projections of the bipartite graph over one of its node sets and apply traditional link prediction methods on the projected graph. Li et al. [19] define a random-walk based kernel function to define the similarity between two types of nodes and predict heterogeneous links in a bipartite graph. The authors of [14, 17, 31] have shown that the link prediction performance improves by utilizing the information such as network structure. But these methods may not work for sparse and weakly clustered networks.

Dunlavy et al. [9] represent the heterogeneous network as a third order tensor and propose a mechanism for collapsing the tensor to matrix and use Katz method to predict links on the matrix. But the tensor based methods are global and time consuming. Cold-start link prediction problem is proposed by Leroy et al. [18]. They predict homogeneous links using the heterogeneous information available in the network.

A meta-path based approach for predicting homogeneous links in a heterogeneous graph is defined in [29]. Meta-path is a sequence of successive homogeneous/heterogeneous edges between two nodes of same type. In [29], Sun et al. propose a measure called *PathSim* between two nodes u and v as the fraction of number of meta-paths between u and v among total paths between u and v. Meta-path selection is a major problem in meta-path based approach. Commonly meta-paths are selected using one of these ways: User may explicitly specify a meta-path combination, best path can be chosen by experiments or training instances can suggest a meta-path. An application of meta-path based approach on bibliographic networks and drug target predictions in chemical networks can be found in [27] and [11] respectively.

2.2   Temporal Link Prediction

The time of formation of a link plays a major role in link prediction. Some measures which utilize temporal information are proposed in [6, 9, 28, 30, 35].

Wang et al. mine the role of an author such as advisor/advisee between two authors by constructing a time-constrained probabilistic factor graph (TPFG) of a coauthorship network [33]. Munasinghe et al. define a measure called time-score [26] for homogeneous networks. Time-score is a neighborhood based measure. A path-based measure called Link-score is defined in [5]. Link-score is the extension of time-score measure for homogeneous networks. A temporal random-walk based extension of Propflow [23], called T_Flow is proposed in [25].

Probabilistic graphical models efficiently utilize the higher order topological information and thus are efficient in link prediction task [32]. Wang et al. propose a measure called Co-occurrence Probability [32](COP) to predict links in homogeneous networks. Lakshmi T.J et al. incorporated time information into COP and obtained better results for predicting homogeneous links in collaboration networks [15]. In this paper, we extend the ideas of COP [32] and TCOP [15] from homogeneous network to heterogeneous network.

Contributions. The contributions made in this paper are

- The proximity-based measures Common Neighbor, Jaccard Coefficient, AdamicAdar [1] and Co-occurrence probability [32] are extended to heterogeneous social networks.
- The temporal measures Time-score [26], Link-score [5], T_Flow [25] and Temporal Co-occurrence Probability [15] are extended to temporal bipartite and heterogeneous social networks.
- The proposed bipartite and heterogeneous link prediction measures are evaluated on two temporal bibliographic networks: DBLP and HiePh treating them as heterogeneous networks.

3   Link Prediction in Heterogeneous Environment

3.1   Problem Statement

Given a ***Temporal Heterogeneous Network*** $G = (V, E, w, t)$, $V = \bigcup\limits_{i=1}^{n} V_i$ represents n types of nodes, $E = \bigcup\limits_{j=1}^{m} E_j$ denotes m types of edges (x, y) where $x \in V_i$, $y \in V_j$, the edge (x, y) is referred to as *homogeneous* if $i = j$ and *heterogeneous* if $i \neq j$. $w : E \rightarrow R, w(x,y)$ denotes the weight of the interaction between x and y and $t : E \rightarrow 2^{\mathbb{N}}$, where $t(x,y)$ is an ordered set of time units denoting the interaction time instants of nodes x and y. We assume a common time unit (encoded as integers) for the entire network.

Temporal Bipartite Network is a special case of Temporal Heterogeneous Network with two types of nodes $V = V_1 \cup V_2$ and purely heterogeneous edges $E \subseteq V_1 \times V_2$.

The aim of **link prediction** between two unconnected nodes $u, v \in \bigcup\limits_{i=1}^{n} V_i$ is to find the possibility of a link of type k, $k \in \{1, 2 \ldots m\}$ appearing between u and v at a future instant of time. Graph G is a homogeneous network if $m = n = 1$ and bipartite if $n = 2$ and $m = 1$.

3.2   Notation

The following notation is followed throughout this paper.

- *Meta-path*: Paths consisting of homogeneous/heterogeneous edges. For example, in Fig. 2(b), $a_1 - a_2$ is a homogeneous edge and $a_1 - c_1 - a_3 - c_3$ is a heterogeneous path.
- $\Gamma_k(u)$: The set of *k-hop* neighbours of node u. $\Gamma_1(u)$ refers to the set of all nodes connected by an edge to u. $\Gamma(u) \cap \Gamma(v)$ denotes the set of common neighbors between node u and v, and $\Gamma_k(u) \cap \Gamma_k(v)$ contains all the common k-hop neighbors between nodes u and v.
- $P_k(u,v)$: The set of meta-paths joining u and v by at most k edges.

3.3   Non-temporal Measures Proposed for Heterogeneous Networks

Heterogeneous networks contain homogeneous as well as meta-paths. Preferential attachment and path based measures can be applied on heterogeneous networks, but common neighborhood based measures cannot be applied directly.

The baseline link prediction measures are extended in heterogeneous environment as follows:

- **Common Neighbours (CN)**: Common neighbors in homogeneous networks as well as heterogeneous networks occur on paths of length 2 between the nodes. For example, in Fig. 3(a), the node $a2$ occurs on path of length 2 between the nodes $a1$ and $a3$, is a common neighbor. Note that in bipartite network in Fig. 3(b), if the edge $a2 - c2$ does not exist, there is no path between the nodes $a1$ and $c1$. Hence for bipartite networks, paths of minimum length 3 have to be considered (Fig. 3(b)) for common neighbour computation. In heterogeneous networks, paths of length 2 as well as 3 exist through homogeneous/heterogeneous edges. Hence, to compute common neighbours in heterogeneous environment, we consider meta-paths of length ≤ 3. This understanding leads to simple definitions that can be extended naturally to

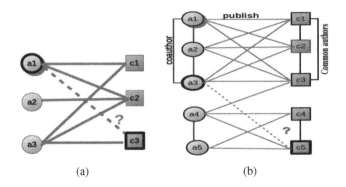

(a)   (b)

Fig. 2. Examples of bipartite and heterogeneous networks

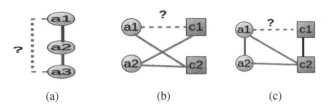

(a)   (b)   (c)

Fig. 3. Minimum length paths containing homogeneous edges (blue and black) and heterogeneous edges (red) between nodes in different types of networks (Color figure online)

Bipartite/heterogeneous environment in contrast to a specialized definition of Adamic Adar for Bipartite networks given in [7].

The common neighbor measure in homogeneous and heterogeneous environments is given as follows:

$$CN(u,v) = |\Gamma_1(u) \bigcap \Gamma_1(v)| \quad \text{in Homogeneous networks}$$
$$= |\Gamma_2(u) \bigcap \Gamma_2(v)| \quad \text{in Bipartite/Heterogeneous networks}$$

(1)

Jaccard Coefficient, AdamicAdar and Preferential Attachment measures are also neighborhood based defined in a similar way as follows.

- **Jaccard Coefficient (JC):** Jaccard Coefficient is the normalized Common Neighbor measure.

$$JC(u,v) = \frac{|\Gamma_1(u) \cap \Gamma_1(v)|}{|\Gamma_1(u) \cup \Gamma_1(v)|} \quad \text{in Homogeneous networks}$$
$$= \frac{|\Gamma_2(u) \cap \Gamma_2(v)|}{|\Gamma_2(u) \cup \Gamma_2(v)|} \quad \text{in Bipartite/Heterogeneous networks}$$

(2)

- **Adamic Adar (AA):**

$$AA(u, v) = \sum_{z \in \Gamma_1(u) \cap \Gamma_1(v)} \frac{1}{log(|\Gamma_1(z)|)} \qquad \text{in Homogeneous networks}$$

$$= \sum_{z \in \Gamma_2(u) \cap \Gamma_2(v)} \frac{1}{log(|\Gamma_2(z)|)} \qquad \text{in Bipartite/Heterogeneous networks} \qquad (3)$$

- **Preferential Attachment (PA):**

$$PA(u, v) = |\Gamma_1(u)| * |\Gamma_1(v)| \qquad \text{in all types of networks} \qquad (4)$$

The proposed measures are summarized in Table 1.

Table 1. Link prediction measures for a node pair (u, v) in various types of networks

LP	Homogeneous networks	Bipartite/heterogeneous networks
CN	$\|\Gamma_1(u) \cap \Gamma_1(v)\|$	$\|\Gamma_2(u) \cap \Gamma_2(v)\|$
JC	$\frac{\|\Gamma_1(u) \cap \Gamma_1(v)\|}{\|\Gamma_1(u) \cup \Gamma_1(v)\|}$	$\frac{\|\Gamma_2(u) \cap \Gamma_2(v)\|}{\|\Gamma_2(u) \cup \Gamma_2(v)\|}$
AA	$\sum_{z \in \Gamma_1(u) \cap \Gamma_1(v)} \frac{1}{log(\|\Gamma_1(z)\|)}$	$\sum_{z \in \Gamma_2(u) \cap \Gamma_2(v)} \frac{1}{log(\|\Gamma_2(z)\|)}$
PA	$\|\Gamma(u)\| * \|\Gamma(v)\|$	$\|\Gamma(u)\| * \|\Gamma(v)\|$

3.4 Temporal Measures Proposed for Heterogeneous Networks

Hetero-Time-Score (Hetero-TS). Let u and v be unconnected nodes in the network. Let p be a path connecting the nodes u and v in $P_3(u, v)$, with edges e lying on p. We extend Time-Score measure proposed for homogeneous networks [26] to heterogeneous environment as follows:

$$Hetero\_TS(u, v) = \sum_{p \in P_3(u,v)} \frac{w(p) * \beta^{r(p)}}{|latest(p) - oldest(p)| + 1} \qquad (5)$$

where $w(p)$ is equal to the harmonic mean of edge weights of edges in p.

β is a damping factor ($0 < \beta < 1$), r is a recency factor, defined as $r(p) = current\_time - \max\limits_{e \ on \ P_3}(t(e))$, $latest(p) = \max\limits_{e \ on \ P_3}(t(e))$ and $oldest(p) = \min\limits_{e \ on \ P_3}(t(e))$.

Hetero-Link-Score (Hetero-LS). Choudhary et al. extend the Time-score measure to obtain a path based measure called Link-score [5]. To obtain the Link-score between two unconnected node u and v, a Time Path Index (TPI) is computed on each path between the nodes u and v. TPI evaluates path weight based on time stamps of links involved in a path. Link-score is the sum of TPI of each path between the nodes u and v.

We extend Link-score to bipartite networks by considering heterogeneous links available in bipartite networks. We also extend Link-score to heterogeneous network by considering meta-paths between two unconnected nodes instead of paths containing only homogeneous links.

Hetero-T_Flow (Hetero-TF). T_Flow [25] is a random-walk based measure, which is an extension of PropFlow measure defined in [23]. T_Flow computes the information flow between two unconnected nodes u and v based on link weights as well as activeness of links by giving more weight to recently formed links.

We extend T_Flow measure to heterogeneous and bipartite networks by considering heterogeneous edges for bipartite networks and both homogeneous and heterogeneous links for heterogeneous networks.

Heterogeneous Temporal Co-occurrence Probability   (Hetero-TCOP). Wang et al. propose a probabilistic measure called Co-occurrence Probability (COP) [32], to predict links in homogeneous networks. $COP(u, v)$ is a joint probability of two unconnected nodes u and v, which involves computation of Markov Random Fields (MRF) of cliques contained in common neighborhood of u and v as described in [32]. Lakshmi T.J et al. incorporated time information into COP and obtained better results for predicting homogeneous links in collaboration networks [15]. We extend the algorithms given in [32] as well as [15] to heterogeneous environment.

We extend $TCOP$ to bipartite and heterogeneous environment by considering complete bipartite subgraphs (B-clique) in the case of bipartite networks and cliques containing homogeneous and heterogeneous edges (H-clique) with regard to heterogeneous networks.

We extend computation of COP in a similar way to Bipartite networks and Heterogeneous networks by extending the computations of clique potentials to B-Cliques and H-cliques respectively. The details of Hetero-TCOP computation in the case of DBLP bibliographic networks are given in Sect. 4.

4   Implementation of Heterogeneous Measures for Bibliographic Networks

Given a **temporal bibliographic graph** $G = (V_a \bigcup V_c, E_{aa} \bigcup E_{ac} \bigcup E_{cc}, w_{aa}, w_{ac}, w_{cc}, t_{aa}, t_{ac}, t_{cc})$, where V_a and V_c represent author and conference nodes respectively and $E_{ij} : V_i \rightarrow V_j$ denotes interaction between nodes of type i and type j respectively. For example, $E_{aa} : V_a \rightarrow V_c$ shows *co-author* relation and E_{ac} *publish* relation. $w_{ij} : E_{ij} \rightarrow \mathbb{N}$ represents weight of edge between node types i and j, with w_{ac} representing the number of papers that the author a publishes in the conference c. And $t_{ij} : E_{ij} \rightarrow 2^{\mathbb{N}}$ represents set of years of interaction between node types i and j.

We discuss prediction of different types of links in bipartite and heterogeneous environments.

- **Prediction of future collaboration of authors (Homogeneous links):** When an author presents a paper in a conference, new interaction with other authors in the same conference may result in new collaborations. This translates to predicting a homogeneous link between $a_1 - a_2$ using the existing heterogeneous links $a_1 - c_1$ and $a_2 - c_1$. We compute the scores based on neighbourhood based extended measures as specified in Table 1.
- **Recommending conferences to authors (Heterogeneous links):** We generate the pairs of author-conference pairs and predict future links by applying the proposed measures. Heterogeneous measures in particular $Hetero - TCOP$ naturally uses these heterogeneous links for link prediction. Now the computation of $Hetero - TCOP$ is explained in detail below.

The implementation of $Hetero\text{-}TCOP$ to compute the score between an author node a_i and a conference node c_j is explained below:

1. **Common neighborhood set of a_i and c_j (CNS(a_i, c_j))** is computed using a breadth first search based algorithm. In this computation, path length is taken as 5 and size of CNS is considered as 6.
2. **Extraction of H-cliques:** Heterogeneous cliques are those that contain nodes of different types and homogeneous as well as heterogeneous edges. Here H-Cliques containing only the nodes of $CNS(a_i, c_j)$ are obtained by the following procedure:

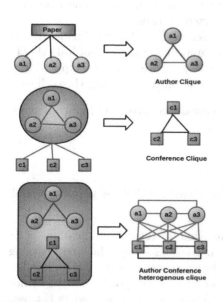

Fig. 4. Extracting heterogeneous cliques from bibliographic network

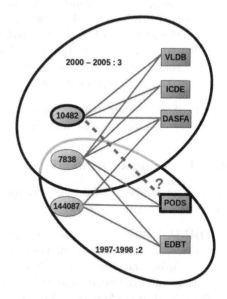

Fig. 5. B-Cliques extracted from DBLP bibliographic network edge labels represent $oldest(x, y) - latest(x, y) : w(x, y)$

- Let A_i be the group of authors who have co-authored with a_i. Finding author cliques is obvious in any network, as the group of authors who publish a paper together can be found in event logs.
- Let C_j be the list of conferences that all the authors in A_i publish.
- Now, $A_i \cup C_j$ forms a heterogeneous clique since all the mutual links among authors and between authors and the corresponding conferences exist.

The extraction of H-Clique containing author nodes and conference nodes is depicted in Fig. 4 and a snapshot of B-cliques extracted is shown in Fig. 5.

3. **Construction of MRF**: MRF construction needs computation of clique potentials. Let F be subsets of H-clique be referred to as factor graphs of H. Clique potential table of a H-clique consists of weights of all its factor graphs F. We define the temporal weight of a factor graph F in a heterogeneous clique H by extending $Hetero - TS$ and $TCOP$ proposed in [15].

$$Temporal-Weight(F) = \frac{w(F).\beta^{r(F)}}{|max(F) - min(F)| + 1} \tag{6}$$

where the definitions of w, r, max_t, min_t are naturally extended to subgraphs F: $w(F)$ is harmonic mean of the edge weights of every edge e in F.
$max_t(F) = \max_{e \in F}(t(e))$ $\beta < 1$ is a damping factor
$min_t(F) = \min_{e \in F}(t(e))$ $r(F) = Current\ Year$ - $max_t(F)$, captures recency of factor F.

An example computation of clique potential table of a H-clique extracted from DBLP bibliographic network is depicted in Table 3.

4. Once the MRF graph is constructed, the $Hetero\text{-}TCOP$ score of nodes a_i and c_j is obtained using junction tree algorithm available in the tool libDAI [24]. Note that $Hetero - TCOP$ score for a link $a_i - c_j$ cannot be computed if a_i and c_j are in disjoint cliques as there exists no path connecting these cliques.

Also note that in heterogeneous environment, coauthor and co-conference homogeneous links are also included.

4.1   Performance Evaluation

We evaluate the extended measures including Hetero-TCOP by performing link prediction for two datasets.

1. **DBLP**: DBLP dataset used in [32] consisting of research publications of 28 conferences in the fields of Data Mining, Databases and Machine Learning held during the years 1997 to 2006. The dataset consists of two types of nodes: author and conference and three types of edges corresponding to co-author links, author-conference links and co-conference links. A link exists between an author node and a conference node, if the author publish a paper in that conference. Co-conference link exists between two conferences, it there are common authors publishing in both conferences.

Table 2. Dataset statistics

	#Nodes		#Edges	
	Author	Conf/jrnl	co-author	author-conf/jrnl
DBLP	23,136	28	56,829	35,665
HiePh	8,381	199	40,736	20,826

2. **HiePh** [22]: HiePh consists of a set of publications in theoretical High Energy Physics during the years 1992–2003. We consider two types of nodes, author and journal and two types of edges, author-author, author-journal and journal-journal.

Details of dataset are shown in Table 2.

4.2 Evaluation Measures

It is a general practice to use Area Under Receiver Operating Characteristic (AUROC) to evaluate the performance of a binary classifier. Area Under Precision Recall (AUPR) curve is considered a more appropriate measure for imbalanced classification problems [8,21]. ROC curves are drawn with FPR (False Positive Rate) against TPR (True Positive Rate) and PR curves are drawn with Recall against Precision. We use AUROC and AUPR for evaluating performance of prediction in this paper.

4.3 Experimental Setting

All the proposed measures along with *Hetero-TCOP* are used as unsupervised measures as well as individual features to form a feature vector in the machine learning framework for link prediction. Every edge is represented as a 9-length feature vector: ($Hetero-CN$, $Hetero-JC$, $Hetero-AA$, $Hetero-PA$, $Hetero-COP$, $Hetero-TS$, $Hetero-LS$, $Hetero-TF$, $Hetero-TCOP$). For bipartite networks, we use the bipartite versions of proposed measures.

Test set is composed of all the edges existing in the last year and the dataset is trained on the network except the last year. For DBLP dataset, the graph of 1997–2005 is taken as training set. The measures are computed on this train set. The performance is evaluated on the test set for pairs of nodes for which edges are formed in the year 2006. The same is the case with HiePh dataset also. The training set is under-sampled and Bagging (10 bags) with Random Forest classification algorithm is used. We used the tool WEKA [12] for Bagging and Random Forest algorithms.

4.4 Results and Discussion

The performance of *Hetero-TCOP* is compared with Hetero-Common Neighbor (CN), Hetero-Jaccard Coefficient (JC), Hetero-Adamic Adar (AA), Hetero-Preferential Attachment (PA), Hetero-Co-occurrence Probability (COP),

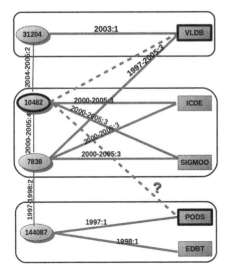

Fig. 6. A snapshot of DBLP heterogeneous network

Table 3. A partial clique potential table ($\phi_C(F)$) of H-clique $C = \{10482, 7838, ICDE, SIGMOD\}$

10482	7838	ICDE	SIGMOD	$\phi_C(F)$
0	0	0	0	0.00000
0	0	0	1	0.00000
...	...	...	...	...
0	1	0	1	0.00000
...	...	...	...	...
0	1	1	0	0.50000
...	...	...	...	...
1	1	0	1	0.50000
1	1	1	0	0.08335
...	...	...	...	...
1	1	1	1	0.08335

Hetero-Time-score (TS), Hetero-Link-score (LS) and Hetero-T_Flow (TF). Similarly, the prediction performance of *Bipartite-TCOP* is compared with all bipartite versions specified in Table 1. The AUROC and AUPR results obtained for DBLP and HiePh datasets are tabulated in Tables 4 and 5 and ROC curves are shown in Figs. 7 and 8.

COP performs best among all the non-temporal measures CN, JC, AA and PA, while TCOP proves to be better over all the temporal as well as non-temporal measures. The proposed *Hetero-TCOP* shows superior performance over all 8 measures for both the datasets.

We analyse a few True Positives discovered by $Hetero - TCOP$ that are missed by COP as well as the other measures; and False Positives of other measures which are rightly rejected by $Hetero - TCOP$.

Consider a snapshot of DBLP heterogeneous network in Fig. 6. DBLP network contains a link between the author node *10482* and the conference node *VLDB* in the year 2006. *Hetero-TCOP* predicts a link between the author *10482* and the conference *VLDB* as the links involved are latest, but the standard link prediction measures compute a low score between *10482* and *VLDB*, as there are more meta-paths of length greater than 2 between them. In the other case, DBLP does not contain a link between the author node *10482* and the conference node *PODS* in the year 2006. Neighborhood-based measures as well as COP predict a link between the author *10482* and the conference *PODS*, as many meta-paths exist between them through author nodes *7838* and *144087* which are old links. *Hetero-TCOP* ranks this low as the links on meta-paths are old.

Table 4. Link prediction performance of author-conf/journal heterogeneous link on **DBLP** and **HiePh** networks

	DBLP				HiePh			
	AUROC		AUPR		AUROC		AUPR	
	Bipartite	Heterogeneous	Bipartite	Heterogeneous	Bipartite	Heterogeneous	Bipartite	Heterogeneous
CN	0.5243	0.5571	0.0014	0.0014	0.5030	0.5350	0.0009	0.0023
JC	0.5019	0.5201	0.0013	0.0015	0.5113	0.5313	0.0013	0.0020
AA	0.6061	0.6370	0.0028	0.0031	0.5521	0.5821	0.0080	0.0036
PA	0.5619	0.5625	0.0015	0.0019	0.5200	0.5326	0.0018	0.0019
COP	0.6861	0.7196	0.0170	0.0129	0.6699	0.6801	0.0110	0.0201
TS	0.6692	0.6783	0.0098	0.0142	0.6313	0.6601	0.0074	0.0091
LS	0.6714	0.6899	0.0132	0.0155	0.6521	0.6712	0.0089	0.0093
TF	0.6790	0.6913	0.0147	0.0193	0.6666	0.6799	0.0094	0.0099
TCOP	**0.7093**	**0.7530**	**0.0251**	**0.0410**	**0.6890**	**0.7104**	**0.0230**	**0.0314**
Supervised	0.7400	0.8120	0.0421	0.0910	0.7395	0.8120	0.04211	0.0910

Table 5. Link prediction performance of co-author relation on **DBLP** and **HiePh** bibliographic networks

	DBLP				HiePh			
	AUROC		AUPR		AUROC		AUPR	
	Homo	Hetero	Homo	Hetero	Homo	Hetero	Homo	Hetero
CN	0.6504	0.6811	0.0681	0.0720	0.5846	0.5920	0.0076	0.0077
JC	0.5942	0.6012	0.0637	0.0660	0.5167	0.5169	0.0045	0.0046
AA	0.6777	0.7011	0.0774	0.0837	0.6064	0.6253	0.0089	0.0094
PA	0.7415	0.7423	0.1162	0.1164	0.5466	0.5500	0.0050	0.0052
COP	0.8379	0.8439	0.2028	0.2399	0.7153	0.7390	0.0215	0.0308
TS	0.7913	0.8290	0.1625	0.1766	0.6752	0.6801	0.0092	0.0105
LS	0.8016	0.8376	0.1721	0.2276	0.6836	0.6900	0.0110	0.0118
TF	0.8125	0.8263	0.1785	0.1791	0.6921	0.7000	0.0114	0.0190
TCOP	**0.8590**	**0.8934**	**0.2421**	**0.3953**	**0.7392**	**0.7575**	**0.0320**	**0.0486**
Supervised	0.9281	0.9420	0.4390	0.5321	0.8396	0.8655	0.0596	0.0688

In the case of author-conference heterogeneous link prediction, all the measures show an improved performance on DBLP/HiePh heterogeneous network over the DBLP/ HiePh bipartite network. More improvement in prediction performance is observed for probabilistic measures COP and TCOP over nonprobabilistic measures in both bipartite and heterogeneous networks. From Table 4, one can see that the performance of *Hetero-TCOP* is improved by 5% over *Bipartite-TCOP* for DBLP network and *Hetero-COP* is improved by 4% over *Bipartite-COP*. Similar is the case with HiePh dataset also. Prediction accuracy is increased in DBLP which is sparse network over the dense network HiePh. In machine learning framework, the prediction accuracy is improved from 74% to 81% for heterogeneous links for DBLP heterogeneous network and from 73% to 81% for HiePh network.

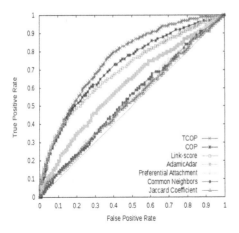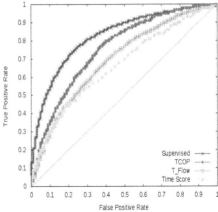

Fig. 7. ROC curve for predicting auth-conf heterogeneous links in DBLP TCOP vs non-temporal measures

Fig. 8. ROC curve for predicting auth-conf heterogeneous links in DBLP TCOP vs temporal measures

In the case of homogeneous (author-author) link prediction, the improvement is less (Table 5). More improvement in the prediction performance is observed for homogeneous links (author-author) when compared to the performance of heterogeneous links (author-conference). *Hetero-TCOP* has shown an accuracy of 9% over neighborhood-based measures and 6% over temporal measures in heterogeneous environment.

An average improvement of around 5% is observed for temporal measures over non-temporal measures, in the prediction of both homogeneous as well as heterogeneous links.

5   Conclusion

Heterogeneous social networks are ubiquitous in nature and contain a lot of hidden information. Most of the state of art link prediction measures project the heterogeneous networks into homogeneous projections and predict homogeneous links. In this work, some of the link prediction measures are extended to heterogeneous environment. A temporal measure called *Hetero-TCOP* is proposed on heterogeneous networks. We evaluate our new measure on two bibliographic networks and predicted two types of links on them. *Hetero-TCOP* demonstrates that taking cognizance of time by differentiating old links from new as well as including heterogeneous information via H-Cliques yields a significant improvement in performance for link prediction.

References

1. Adamic, L.A., Adar, E.: Friends and neighbors on the web. Soc. Netw. **25**, 211–230 (2001)
2. Benchettara, N., Kanawati, R., Rouveirol, C.: Supervised machine learning applied to link prediction in bipartite social networks. In: 2010 International Conference on Advances in Social Networks Analysis and Mining (ASONAM), pp. 326–330. IEEE (2010)
3. Berlusconi, G., Calderoni, F., Parolini, N., Verani, M., Piccardi, C.: Link prediction in criminal networks: a tool for criminal intelligence analysis. PLOS ONE **4**, 1–21 (2016)
4. Breiman, L.: Bagging predictors. Mach. Learn. **24**(2), 123–140 (1996)
5. Choudhary, P., Mishra, N., Sharma, S., Patel, R.: Link score: a novel method for time aware link prediction in social network. In: ICDMW (2013)
6. da Silva Soares, P.R., Prudêncio, R.B.C.: Time series based link prediction. In: The 2012 International Joint Conference on Neural Networks (IJCNN), pp. 1–7. IEEE (2012)
7. Davis, D.A., Lichtenwalter, R., Chawla, N.V.: Supervised methods for multi-relational link prediction. Soc. Netw. Anal. Min. **3**(2), 127–141 (2013)
8. Davis, J., Goadrich, M.: The relationship between precision-recall and ROC curves. In: Proceedings of the 23rd International Conference on Machine Learning, ICML 2006, pp. 233–240 (2006)
9. Dunlavy, D.M., Kolda, T.G., Acar, E.: Temporal link prediction using matrix and tensor factorizations. ACM Trans. Knowl. Discov. Data (TKDD) **5**(2), 10 (2011)
10. Fire, M., Puzis, R., Elovici, Y.: Link Prediction in Highly Fractional Data Sets, pp. 283–300. Springer, New York (2013)
11. Gang, F., Ding, Y., Seal, A., Chen, B., Sun, Y., Bolton, E.: Predicting drug target interactions using meta-path-based semantic network analysis. BMC Bioinform. **17**(1), 1 (2016)
12. Hall, M., Frank, E., Holmes, G., Pfahringer, B., Reutemann, P., Witten, I.H.: The WEKA data mining software: an update. SIGKDD Explor. Newsl. **11**(1), 10–18 (2009)
13. Al Hasan, M., Chaoji, V., Salem, S., Zaki, M.: Link prediction using supervised learning. In: Proceedings of SDM 2006 Workshop on Link Analysis, Counter-Terrorism and Security (2006)
14. Jaya Lakshmi, T., Durga Bhavani, S.: Enhancement to community-based multi-relational link prediction using co-occurrence probability feature. In: Proceedings of the Second ACM IKDD Conference on Data Sciences, CoDS 2015, pp. 86–91. ACM (2015)
15. Jaya Lakshmi, T., Durga Bhavani, S.: Temporal probabilistic measure for link prediction in collaborative networks. Appl. Intell. 1–13 (2017)
16. Katz, L.: A new status index derived from sociometric analysis. Psychometrika **18**(1), 39–43 (1953)
17. Jaya Lakshmi, T., Durga Bhavani, S.: Heterogeneous link prediction based on multi relational community information. In: Sixth International Conference on Communication Systems and Networks, COMSNETS 2014, pp. 1–4 (2014)
18. Leroy, V., Cambazoglu, B.B., Bonchi, F.: Cold start link prediction. In: Proceedings of the 16th ACM SIGKDD International Conference on Knowledge Discovery and Data Mining, pp. 393–402. ACM (2010)

19. Li, X., Chen, H.: Recommendation as link prediction in bipartite graphs: a graph kernel-based machine learning approach. Decis. Support Syst. **54**(2), 880–890 (2013)
20. Liben-Nowell, D., Kleinberg, J.: The link-prediction problem for social networks. J. Am. Soc. Inf. Sci. Technol. **58**(7), 1019–1031 (2007)
21. Lichtenwalter, R., Chawla, N.V.: Link prediction: fair and effective evaluation. In: ASONAM, pp. 376–383. IEEE Computer Society (2012)
22. Lichtenwalter, R.N., Chawla, N.V.: Vertex collocation profiles: theory, computation, and results. SpringerPlus **3**(1), 1–27 (2014)
23. Lichtenwalter, R.N., Lussier, J.T., Chawla, N.V.: New perspectives and methods in link prediction. In: Proceedings of the 16th ACM SIGKDD International Conference on Knowledge Discovery and Data Mining, KDD 2010, pp. 243–252. ACM (2010)
24. Mooij, J.M.: libDAI: a free and open source C++ library for discrete approximate inference in graphical models. J. Mach. Learn. Res. **11**, 2169–2173 (2010)
25. Munasinghe, L.: Time-aware methods for link prediction in social networks. Ph.D. thesis, The Graduate University for Advanced Studies (2013)
26. Munasinghe, L., Ichise, R.: Time aware index for link prediction in social networks. In: Cuzzocrea, A., Dayal, U. (eds.) DaWaK 2011. LNCS, vol. 6862, pp. 342–353. Springer, Heidelberg (2011). doi:10.1007/978-3-642-23544-3_26
27. Sun, Y., Barber, R., Gupta, M., Aggarwal, C.C., Han, J.: Co-author relationship prediction in heterogeneous bibliographic networks. In: Proceedings of the 2011 International Conference on Advances in Social Networks Analysis and Mining, ASONAM 2011, pp. 121–128. IEEE Computer Society (2011)
28. Sun, Y., Han, J., Aggarwal, C.C., Chawla, N.V.: When will it happen? Relationship prediction in heterogeneous information networks. In: Proceedings of the Fifth ACM International Conference on Web Search and Data Mining, pp. 663–672. ACM (2012)
29. Sun, Y., Han, J., Yan, X., Yu, P.S., Wu, T.: Pathsim: meta path-based top-k similarity search in heterogeneous information networks. Proc. VLDB Endow. **4**(11), 992–1003 (2011)
30. Tylenda, T., Angelova, R., Bedathur, S.: Towards time-aware link prediction in evolving social networks. In: Proceedings of the 3rd Workshop on Social Network Mining and Analysis, SNA-KDD 2009, pp. 1–10. ACM (2009)
31. Valverde-Rebaza, J.C., Andrade Lopes, A.: Link prediction in complex networks based on cluster information. In: Barros, L.N., Finger, M., Pozo, A.T., Gimenénez-Lugo, G.A., Castilho, M. (eds.) SBIA 2012. LNCS (LNAI), pp. 92–101. Springer, Heidelberg (2012). doi:10.1007/978-3-642-34459-6_10
32. Wang, C., Satuluri, V., Parthasarathy, S.: Local probabilistic models for link prediction. In: Proceedings of Seventh IEEE International Conference on Data Mining, ICDM 2007, pp. 322–331. IEEE Computer Society (2007)
33. Wang, C., Han, J., Jia, Y., Tang, J., Zhang, D., Yu, Y., Guo, J.: Mining advisor-advisee relationships from research publication networks. In: Proceedings of the 16th ACM SIGKDD International Conference on Knowledge Discovery and Data Mining, KDD 2010, pp. 203–212. ACM (2010)
34. Wang, P., BaoWen, X., YuRong, W., Zhou, X.Y.: Link prediction in social networks: the state-of-the-art. Sci. China Inf. Sci. **1**(58), 1–38 (2015)
35. Yang, Y., Chawla, N.V., Sun, Y., Han, J.: Predicting links in multi-relational and heterogeneous networks. In: 12th IEEE International Conference on Data Mining, ICDM 2012, Brussels, 10–13 December 2012, pp. 755–764 (2012)

NetRating: Credit Risk Evaluation for Loan Guarantee Chain in China

Xiangfeng Meng, Yunhai Tong$^{(\boxtimes)}$, Xinhai Liu, Yiren Chen, and Shaohua Tan

Key Laboratory of Machine Perception, Center for Information Science,
Peking University, Beijing 100871, China
`pku.ericmeng@foxmail.com`, `yhtong@pku.edu.cn`

Abstract. Guaranteed loans are a common way for enterprises to raise money from banks without any collateral in China. The enterprises are highly intertwined with each other, and hence form a densely connected guarantee network. As the economy is down in recent years, the default risk spreads along with the guarantee relations, and has caused great financial risk in many regions of China. Thus it puts forward a new challenge for financial regulators to monitor the enterprises involved in the guarantee network and control the system risk. However, the traditional financial risk management are based on vector space models, and could not handle the relations among enterprises. In this paper, based on the k-shell decomposition method, we propose a novel risk evaluation strategy, NetRating, to assess the risk level of each enterprise involved in the guaranteed loans. Besides, to deal with the direct guarantee networks, we propose the directed k-shell decomposition method, and extend NetRating strategy to the directed NetRating strategy. The application of our strategy in the real data verifies its effectiveness in credit assessment. It indicates that our strategy can provide a novel perspective for financial regulators to monitor the guarantee networks and control potential system risk.

Keywords: Enterprise monitoring · Risk control · Credit rating · Guarantee relation · Netrating · The k-shell decomposition method

1 Introduction

As the financial system is not developed in China, bank loan has been a popular approach for enterprises to raise money. As the cost of assessing whether these enterprises have good credit is high in the absence of collateral, banks are reluctant to extend loans without explicit backing. Thus these enterprises have to seek for other enterprises to back loans for them. It is said that around a quarter of loans in China's bank system are backed by such guarantees.

Usually, enterprises involved in guaranteed loans are closely intertwined, thus forming the so-called loan guarantee chain. With the decline of Chinese economy in the recent years, loan guarantee chain of enterprises has become a big issue for Chinese financial system as increasing number of enterprises, from Yangtze

© Springer International Publishing AG 2017
G.A. Wang et al. (Eds.): PAISI 2017, LNCS 10241, pp. 99–108, 2017.
DOI: 10.1007/978-3-319-57463-9_7

River Delta to Circum-Bohai-Sea region, are deeply involved. This financial phenomenon, like an epidemic disease, is spreading over time and thus threatening the stability of Chinese financial system. So it is urgent for financial regulators to monitor the enterprises and prevent further risk spreading.

Though economists have proposed multiple approaches, these approaches have a major drawback. They describe and predict the credit risk of entities by extracting features of each entity, such as consumer or enterprises, while neglecting the interdependencies within the credit entities. Thus, more systemic analysis is required for tacking the credit risk caused by loan guarantee chain.

Fortunately, network science provides a powerful tool to analyze the correlations among entities. Previous studies have combined financial applications with complex network theory [2,5,6,8,12]. For instance, Allen and Babus [1] gave multiple kinds of financial networks and described the empirical results of them; Galbiati, Delpini and Battiston [7] tried to analyze the controllability of financial systems by using complex network.

In this paper, we propose a network-based analytic framework to deal with the loan guarantee chain and help regulators monitor the evolution of the guarantee chain. We leverage the complex network theory to model the loan guarantee chain. The enterprises are modeled as nodes while the loan guarantee relations are the links among them. We put forward a new type of credit risk (we define it as outer credit risk). It integrates both the relation structure information and the loan default reality. With collaboration with People's Bank of China, which collects the loan guarantee data nationwide, we test the validity of our methods through the data from real loan guarantee chain. Verified by both the numerical evaluation and risk analysis, our strategy could help solve the complicated credit risk management of loan guarantee chain.

The contributions of this paper are two-fold. First, we model the loan guarantee chain by using complex network theory. It is believed that the network based analysis of the loan guarantee chain will provide more insights about the system risk caused by credit default. Second, we present a novel network based credit rating strategy to measure the credit worthiness of enterprises involved in the loan guarantee chain. We apply this novel strategy to the data set of guarantee loans in China. Numerical evaluations demonstrate that this novel strategy could depict the worthiness of enterprises accurately.

The rest of this paper is organized as follows. Related works about the researches of guaranteed loans are introduced in Sect. 2. The novel credit rating strategy, named 'NetRating', is formulated in Sect. 3. The data set adopted in this paper and the experimental results are presented in Sect. 4. We give the conclusion in Sect. 5.

2   Related Works

2.1   Researches About the Guarantee Chain in China

As loan guarantee is crucial for financial system in China, some Chinese scholars have conducted such kind of researches. Zhang [16] introduced the guarantee chain crisis, analyzed its infecting process and modeled the critical condition with infection models. The strategy relies on the vector based dynamic equation and the simulation process is implemented. Zhang [10] gave a basis analysis about the risk sharing mechanism, the risk reduction mechanism and risk contagions of the guarantee chain. The conclusion is that risk sharing was beneficial in a favorable economic environment but risk contagion would lead all companies in trouble in a difficult environment. Leng, Zhang and Xing [11] adopted regression models to analyze the transfer of risk to guarantors by using the data set of the listed Chinese companies that have issued bonds. The results showed that if risk is well managed, the provision of loan guarantees does not affect the default risk of guarantors. However, when a guarantor firm is controlled by the government, the provision of guarantees increases the firm's default risk.

2.2   Researches About the Financial Networks

Recently network analysis has attracted more attentions in the financial field. In 2013, Nature physics delivered a special issue named 'Complex Network in Finance'. It believes that thanks to the ability to interpret the network parameters with respect to stability, robustness and efficiency of an underlying system, financial networks have become a natural candidate to study. The financial system can be thought as a set of intermediaries, such as banks that interact with each other through financial transactions. These interactions are governed by a set of rules and regulations, and take place on an interaction graph of all connections between financial intermediaries.

Battison et al. [4] introduced DebtRank, a novel measurement of the systemic impact inspired by feedback-centrality. It measures the systemically important institutions in a financial network extracted from the USD 1.2 trillion FED emergency loans program. Vitali [15] investigated the architecture of the control network consisting of transnational corporations. These corporations could affect both the competitions in global markets and financial stability. Thus how to find the core financial institutions, which can be seen as an economic "super-entity", becomes a new important issue for both researchers and policy makers. Van Vlasselaer et al. [14] employed social network analysis to detect the fraud transactions during financial paying.

2.3   Traditional Financial Risk Management

In traditional credit risk management, the financial entities are described by vector space based features. Some features are directly from the following properties: Character, Capital, Collateral, Capability, Condition and Stability. Other features are derived from the original features through linear combinations or other approaches. One classical model for quantifying the credit risk is linear regression. For instance, Eq. 1 shows a classical regression model when measuring the credit risk:

$$R = k_1 * x_1 + k_2 * x_2 + \ldots + k_n * x_n + b, \tag{1}$$

where R represents the risk assessment of an enterprise, $\{x_1, \ldots, x_n\}$ denotes the feature vector of an enterprise, $\{k_1, k_2, \ldots, k_n, b\}$ is the coefficient vector. The traditional credit risk strategy works well when predicting the default risk as long as the training data is rich enough.

However, for enterprises that have close relationships with other enterprises, such as the family relation, group relation, upstream/downstream relation and loan guarantee relation, credit behavior could not depict their risk profiles alone. These relations can also lead to risk diffusions among them, although the mechanism is quite complicated compared to the traditional credit risk measurements. So we need to seek a new scheme to model the relations among enterprises to measure the inherent risk.

3   Methodologies

3.1   Credit Rating

Credit rating is designed to provide information about credit quality [9,13]. It describes the evaluation of the credit worthiness of a debtor. Credit rating has a direct effect on equity prices, bond prices and risk management strategies. For instance, given the credit rating of corporations, individuals are informed of the likelihood that the corporations will pay their obligations.

However, these traditional approaches suffer from a major drawback. Though credit rating results from a thorough analysis of both public and private information from various relevant sources, these approaches treat each financial entity individually, and neglect the correlations within different financial entities. In fact, financial entities exhibit a high degree of interdependence. Mother companies and subsidiary companies are directly connected through cross shareholding. Upstream enterprises and downstream enterprises are directly connected through the transfer of both products and funds. Thus the default of one company may lead to wide spread of defaults along with the interdependent connections. How the connections within financial agents affect their credit ratings remains a problem.

3.2   NetRating Based on the k-shell Decomposition Method

As discussed in the previous part, the traditional credit rating strategy does not work well for assessing the financial risk caused by loan guarantee relations. Meanwhile, complex network analysis provides many useful tools for statistic and calculation. This paper applies the network theory to the loan guarantee networks, and puts forward a method named NetRating to assess the credit risk of enterprises caused by loan guarantee relations.

The NetRating strategy is based on the k-shell decomposition method. The k-shell decomposition method partitions a network into sub-structures that are directly linked to centrality [3]. This method assigns an integer index, ks, to each node, which indicates the location of the node in the network according to its connectivity patterns. Nodes with low/high values of ks are located at the periphery/center of the network. This way, the network is described by a layered structure that reveals the full hierarchy of its nodes. The innermost nodes belong to the structure are called cores or "nucleus" of the network, while the remaining nodes are placed into more external layers (k-shells).

Concerning the loan guarantee network, if an enterprise is a core in the network, its risk level might be high as more enterprises are attached to it. Also, it is easy to spread the credit risk into the other part of the network, thus leading to system risk. So the k-shell index of an enterprise is related to its risk level. We can obtain the credit risk rating of an enterprise based on the k-shell index of the enterprise. As this rating scheme is based on network analysis, we denote it as NetRating.

The detailed procedures of the NetRating strategy are as follows. First, we removes enterprises from the loan guarantee network with degree $k = 1$, and assigns the integer $ks = 1$ to them. This step is repeatedly carried out until the degree of any remaining enterprise is above 1. Then, enterprises with degrees $k = 2$ are removed from the loan guarantee network and are assigned the integer $ks = 2$. This step will be repeated again until the degrees of remaining nodes are above 2. Similar procedures are repeated for nodes with degrees $k \geq 3$ until all the enterprises are assigned a ks value.

Figure 1 shows the risk measurement of enterprises by the NetRating strategy. In Fig. 1, 19 enterprises form a loan guarantee network because of their loan guarantee relationships. The k-shell decomposition method is run on this network to obtain the k-shell index for each enterprise. It can be seen that the set of enterprises within the innermost ring occupy the largest ks value, with $ks = 3$. The set of enterprises between the two outermost rings have the smallest ks value, with $ks = 1$. Particularly, even though the 11th enterprise has the largest degree, with $k = 6$, its ks value is still 1, because the enterprises linked to it are single nodes. Thus it is not a core node in the network.

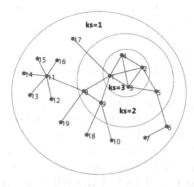

Fig. 1. Visualization of k-shell based NetRating scheme

It needs to mention that the current k-shell index is not the real credit risk grade in the application of credit risk management. We will discuss the transformation in Sect. 4.

3.3 NetRating Based on the Directed k-shell Decomposition Method

In the loan guarantee network, links between each pair of enterprises are direct, which means that one enterprise backs the other enterprise to get bank loans. For instance, Fig. 2 depicts a directed network, of which the symmetrical version is the same as the undirected network shown in Fig. 1. In Fig. 2, the 7th enterprise is guaranteed by the 6th enterprise, and the 17th enterprise guarantee for the 1st enterprise. In such situation, the 7th enterprise should be free from potential outer credit risk as it does not back for any enterprise, while the 17th enterprise should suffer from potential outer credit risk as it backs for many enterprises and have to face great default threats.

However, the ks values of these two enterprises (the 7th and 17th companies) in the NetRating strategy are identical, which is inconsistent to the intuition. Motivated by this problem, we propose the directed k-shell decomposition method and extend the NetRating strategy based on the novel directed k-shell decomposition method.

In this paper, we propose the directed NetRating scheme. The basic principle is that two enterprises (We suppose they are A and B) along an edge in the loan guarantee network are exposed with different kinds of risk: the enterprise A starting the edge will suffer from the potential outer credit risk from enterprise B while the enterprise B pointed by the edge will not. Consequently, the enterprises starting the edges will be taken into consideration for risk assessment in our strategy. In terms of complex network analysis, the out-degree of an enterprise is taken into account while the in-degree of an enterprise is neglected.

This novel method applies a similar pruning routine as the standard k-shell decomposition method, but is based on an alternative measure of nodes' degrees and an alternative initial step.

First, as the credit risk is diffused along with the inverse directions of edges, the out-degrees of enterprises are considered in directed k-shell decomposition method. Second, when the out-degrees of some enterprises are 0, these enterprises are free from the potential outer credit risk caused by risk diffusions. So the ks values of these enterprises are set as the minimum value 0.

We re-calculate the k-shell structure of the directed network in Fig. 2, and show the result in Fig. 3, where different colors represent different ks values that the nodes take. After calculating NetRating, we get three types of k-shell index. Green nodes represent the guaranteed enterprises and their ks values are 0. The ks value of blue nodes is 1, and that of the yellow nodes is 2. Compared with that in Fig. 1, we can find that due to the dense connections between the first four nodes labeled as 1, 2, 3 and 4, they remain the core nodes in this network. Particularly, the 17th node is more important than above, as it backs a central

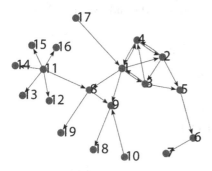
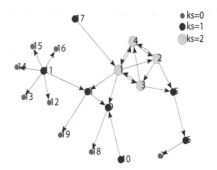

Fig. 2. The illustration of a loan guarantee network

Fig. 3. The credit rating of enterprises by directed NetRating method (Color figure online)

node, which indicates that it will face more outer credit risk threats; while under the undirected NetRating, its k-shell index is the smallest.

The analysis of the directed network in Fig. 3 shows that the directed k-shell decomposition method yields a more refined partitioning of the directed networks as it utilizes more information from the loan guarantee network. Besides, nodes that initially lie at the peripheral of the networks identified by the standard k-shell decomposition method are likely to be more close to the cores of networks.

4   Experiments

4.1   Data Set and Pre-processing

The financial data set adopted in this research is obtained from one commercial bank in China. It contains the records of bank loans that are guaranteed by other companies within twelve adjacent months during 2007. Among each record of the bank loans, the relevant information about enterprise that raises money from bank, enterprise that backs for the bank loan and the details of the bank loan are provided. The bank loan guarantee networks can be constructed with nodes representing companies and direct edges representing the guarantee relations.

4.2   Evaluation of the NetRating Strategy

In this section, we will evaluate whether the NetRating strategy could accurately measure the outer credit worthiness of companies involved in the guarantee networks. As mentioned before, the k-shell index of each enterprise is not identical to its credit ratings, it is necessary to do some transformations. In this experiment, before verifying the effectiveness of our strategy, we implement the transformation as shown in Table 1 for the undirected NetRating scheme.

Regarding how to verify the effectiveness of the novel network-based credit rating strategy, the intuitive way is to detect how many enterprises with weak

Table 1. Mappings from the ks values to the credit grades for the undirected NetRating scheme

ks	Credit grade	Credit quality
1	A	Strong
2	B	Adequate
3	C	Speculative
4	D	Vulnerable

Table 2. Prediction evaluation of NetRating based on the standard k-shell decomposition method

Credit grade	Company number	Default rate (half-year)	Default rate (1-year)
A (ks=0)	3452	0.93%	1.25%
B (ks=1)	2328	2.28%	2.96%
C (ks=2)	428	5.84%	8.41%
D (ks=3)	61	0	0

credit ratings will default in the following periods. In our research, 13 temporal guarantee networks can be constructed. For simplicity, we apply our novel method to the first snapshot of the temporal guarantee networks, and evaluate the results of the novel method by using the remaining 12 snapshots of the temporal guarantee networks. In other words, we will check how many enterprises with weak credit ratings will default in both the following half a year observation window and the following one year observation window.

Table 2 shows the assessment result of our NetRating scheme based on the standard k-shell decomposition. In Table 2, it can be seen that for the first three credit grades, 'A', 'B' and 'C', the default rate increases while the credit grades degenerate. Especially for the credit grade 'C', the default rate in the next one year, 8.41%, is remarkably high while the default ratio of enterprises with credit grade 'A' is only 1.25%. It seems that our strategy does not work well for enterprises with credit grade 'D'. There are two reasons: the number of these enterprises is small; the edge directionality is not full employed.

4.3 Evaluation of the Directed NetRating Strategy

In this section, we evaluate whether the directed NetRating strategy could accurately measure the outer credit worthiness of companies involved in the guarantee networks, and that whether the directed NetRating strategy performs better than the NetRating strategy.

We implement the transformation as shown in Table 3 for the directed NetRating scheme. Table 4 shows the assessment result of our NetRating scheme based on the directed k-shell decomposition method. The default rate of

Table 3. Mappings from the ks values to the credit grades for the directed NetRating scheme

ks	Credit grade	Credit quality
1	A	Strong
2	B	Weak
3	C	Vulnerable

Table 4. Prediction evaluation of NetRating based on the directed k-shell method

Credit grade	Company number	Default rate (half-year)	Default rate (1-year)
A (ks=0)	5959	1.66%	2.25%
B (ks=1)	299	2.01%	2.68%
C (ks=2)	11	45.45%	54.55%

companies with credit grade 'A' is the lowest, followed by that of companies with 'B', and the default rate of companies with 'C' are the largest. To be more detailed, only 1.66% of the companies with 'A' default in the next half a year, and 2.25% of these companies default in the next year. 199 companies are assigned with credit grade 'B', with 2.01% of them defaults in the next half a year and 2.68% default in the next year. The credit grades of 11 companies are 'C', indicating that these 11 companies are most likely to default in the future. As is shown in Table 4, 45.45% of these companies default in the next half a year, and 54.55% default in the next year.

Thus, the directed NetRating strategy is effective in approximate the worthiness of enterprises. By considering the edge directionality, the obtained credit ratings of enterprises are more meaningful.

5   Conclusions

To quantitatively measure the potential credit risk of enterprises that is caused by default risk spreading, we put forward a new strategy named NetRating. Besides, considering the directionality of the guarantee networks, we propose the directed k-shell decomposition method, and extend the NetRating strategy to directed NetRating strategy. The novel strategy has the following merits. First, it is based on the complex network theory, and is able to deal with complex relational data set. Second, the directed NetRating strategy can effectively depict how susceptible the enterprises are when exposed to external default risk. The experiment on the real data has verified the effectiveness of our strategy. It shows that our NetRating strategy is able to provide a new risk analytic tool for loan guarantee related risk management.

Thus the directed NetRating strategy provides an effective tool for financial regulators to monitor the guarantee networks and control potential system risk.

Given the credit risk an enterprise is exposed due to the external default risk spreading, both the financial regulators and the governments are able to monitor the worthiness of the enterprise in time, and prevent the outbreak of system risk.

The novel strategy is just a starting point to explore the risk management of guaranteed loan. As a later study, we will investigate the combination of external risk and internal risk, aiming at depicting the worthiness of enterprises more comprehensively. This will provide more powerful analysis tool for financial regulators to monitor the potential system risk in guarantee networks.

References

1. Allen, F., Babus, A.: Networks in finance (2008)
2. Allen, F., Babus, A., Carletti, E.: Financial connections and systemic risk. Technical report, National Bureau of Economic Research (2010)
3. Batagelj, V., Zaveršnik, M.: Fast algorithms for determining (generalized) core groups in social networks. Adv. Data Anal. Classif. 5(2), 129–145 (2011)
4. Battiston, S., Puliga, M., Kaushik, R., Tasca, P., Caldarelli, G.: Debtrank: Too central to fail? financial networks, the FED and systemic risk. Sci. Rep. 2, 541 (2012). Nature Publishing Group
5. Caldarelli, G., Chessa, A., Pammolli, F., Gabrielli, A., Puliga, M.: Reconstructing a credit network. Nat. Phys. 9(3), 125–126 (2013)
6. Gai, P., Kapadia, S.: Contagion in financial networks. In: Proceedings of the Royal Society of London A: Mathematical, Physical and Engineering Sciences, p. rspa20090410. The Royal Society (2010)
7. Galbiati, M., Delpini, D., Battiston, S.: The power to control. Nat. Phys. 9(3), 126–128 (2013)
8. Glasserman, P., Young, H.P.: How likely is contagion in financial networks? J. Bank. Finance 50, 383–399 (2015)
9. Hull, J.C.: Risk Management and Financial Institutions, vol. 733. John Wiley & Sons, Hoboken (2012). + Web Site
10. Le-cai, Z.: Financial security chain of enterprises: risk reduction, risk contagion and risk sharing - a case study on financial security chain of enterprises in Zhejiang. Econ. Theor. Bus. Manage. 10, 006 (2011)
11. Leng, A., Zhang, J., Xing, G.: Loan guarantees and guarantor default risk: Evidence from china. Management Review (2014). (In CHINESE), Forthcoming
12. Nier, E., Yang, J., Yorulmazer, T., Alentorn, A.: Network models and financial stability. J. Econ. Dyn. Control 31(6), 2033–2060 (2007)
13. Van Gestel, T., Baesens, B.: Credit Risk Management: Basic Concepts: Financial Risk Components, Rating Analysis, Models Economic and Regulatory Capital. Oxford University Press, New York (2008)
14. Van Vlasselaer, V., Meskens, J., Van Dromme, D., Baesens, B.: Using social network knowledge for detecting spider constructions in social security fraud. In: 2013 IEEE/ACM International Conference on Advances in Social Networks Analysis and Mining (ASONAM), pp. 813–820. IEEE (2013)
15. Vitali, S., Glattfelder, J.B., Battiston, S.: The network of global corporate control (2011)
16. Zhang, Z.-X., Li, P.-X., Guo, J.-E.: The infection mechanism of the guarantee chain crisis [j]. Syst. Eng. 4, 005 (2012)

Information Access and Security

VQ Coding in Data Hiding Using Correlated Neighboring Blocks in Security Performance

Cheng-Ta Huang[1], De-En Sun[2], Yen-Lin Chen[3], and Shiuh-Jeng Wang[2([⊠])]

[1] Department of Information Management,
Oriental Institute of Technology, New Taipei City, Taiwan
[2] Department of Information Management,
Central Police University, Taoyuan, Taiwan
`sjwang@mail.cpu.edu.tw`
[3] Information Cryptology Construction Laboratory,
Department of Information Management, Central Police University,
Taoyuan, Taiwan

Abstract. With the continued expansion of the Internet and increased means of communication, it is inevitable that we send data via the Internet or other such media. The important issue of maintaining the confidentiality and integrity of such data when using the Internet as a primary mode of communication also continues to grow in scale. In this paper, we therefore propose an information-hiding method based on the vector quantization (VQ) compression algorithm with elastic indicators; further, we present our design for a key stream to enhance security. Our experimental results have shown that our proposed method performs better as compared to the method introduced by Lee et al. in 2013.

Keywords: Vector quantization · Information hiding · Image compression · Huffman coding · Elastic indicator

1 Introduction

For decades, researchers have developed information hiding techniques to protect the confidentiality and integrity of messages sent to one another. With the continued growth of the Internet, the use of digital information and digital images has increased dramatically, which further emphasizes the importance of maintaining the confidentiality and integrity of transmitted information. General methods to protect secret information are typically divided into two categories, i.e., cryptography and information hiding. The main purpose of cryptography is to avoid unauthorized individuals from seeing the secret information, whereas the main purpose of information hiding is to ensure unauthorized individuals are not aware that secret information is hidden within other media, such as video, image, and text files.

Information hiding techniques using images are divided into three categories, i.e., spatial domain approaches [1–7], frequency domain approaches [8–11],

© Springer International Publishing AG 2017
G.A. Wang et al. (Eds.): PAISI 2017, LNCS 10241, pp. 111–128, 2017.
DOI: 10.1007/978-3-319-57463-9_8

and compression domain approaches [12–14]. Information hiding in the spatial domain is the most intuitive; here, algorithms are designed to directly modify pixel values, using such methods as least significant bit (LSB) [1,2], difference expansion (DE) [3–5], and histogram modification [6,7]. If the robustness of the transmitted data is a top priority, algorithms are often applied to the frequency domain, including discrete cosines transform (DCT) methods [8–10] and discrete wavelet transform (DWT) methods [11]. If the efficiency of data transmission over the Internet is a top priority, information hiding algorithms based on the compression domain are often applied, including vector quantization (VQ) coding [15]. In general, VQ information hiding methods [12–14] are further classified into three categories according to their output format; these categories are VQ image methods, VQ-based image methods with control messages, and codestream-based methods.

Given the above, in this paper, we propose an information hiding model based on VQ coding between correlated neighboring blocks. Our proposed model is applicable to codestream-based VQ information hiding methods. Goals of our proposed model are to improve security and find optimal parameters for encoding and decoding using Huffman coding.

The remainder of our paper is organized as follows. In Sect. 2, we introduce some background information and related work, including such topics as VQ coding [15], Huffman coding [16] and Lee et al.'s data hiding method [12]. Next, we present our proposed elastic indicator VQ information hiding method in Sect. 3. Section 4 shows our experimental results and analysis. Finally, in Sect. 5, we present our conclusions and provide avenues for future work.

2   Related Work

In this section, we present VQ coding and Huffman coding in Sect. 2.1 and Sect. 2.2, respectively. We then describe the codestream-based VQ information hiding method developed by Lee et al. [12] in Sect. 2.3.

2.1   Vector Quantization (VQ)

VQ, also known as block quantization, is often used for lossy data compression, encoding values from a multidimensional vector space to a finite set of lower-dimensional values that thereby occupies less storage space and leads to a higher data compression ratio. A VQ coding algorithm consists of three parts, i.e., codebook generation, image encoding, and image decoding.

The most commonly used method for generating a codebook is the Linde-Buzo-Gray (LBG) algorithm [15], proposed by Linde, Buzo, and Gray in 1980. This algorithm selects some featured blocks from non-overlapping blocks of certain images. A codebook is then composed of these featured blocks, which are called codewords; here, pixel values of a featured block are the components of a codeword. Each codeword has its own index value, which depends on codebook size. The first step of VQ encoding is to divide the cover image into several

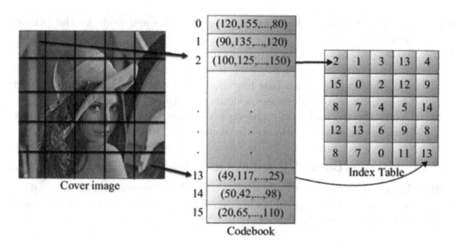

Fig. 1. The VQ encoding procedure.

non-overlapping blocks. Next, all blocks are encoded using the similar codeword in the codebook and calculating the Euclidean distance. More specifically, the Euclidean distance is calculated via Eq. (1), where u represents the pixel value of the block, v represents the pixel value of the codeword, and k is the size of the codeword. Thus, we have:

$$d(u,v) = \sum_{i=1}^{k}(u_i - v_i)^2 \tag{1}$$

All non-overlapping blocks of the cover image are encoded using the codewords with the smallest Euclidean distance. The corresponding index value of the nearest distance codeword serves as the output as VQ encodes an image block. The finial output is then an index table. Figure 1 illustrates this VQ encoding procedure.

2.2   Huffman Code

The Huffman code is an optimal prefix code commonly used for lossless data compression that was originally proposed by Huffman [16]. The output from Huffman's algorithm is a variable-length code table used to encode source symbols, with the more frequently used symbols generally represented using fewer bits than the less frequently used symbols. To achieve this, Huffman coding derives a frequency table from the frequency of occurrences for each possible value of the source symbol, then creates a binary tree of nodes.

This tree can be traversed backwards, from right to left, assigning different bits to different branches. The specific construction algorithm using a priority queue is described below.

Step 1: Create a leaf node for each symbol; add the leaf node to the priority queue.

Step 2: Remove the two nodes with the highest priority from the queue, then create a new internal node with these two nodes as children; the probability associated with this new node is the sum of the two child node probabilities. Add this new node to the priority queue.

Step 3: Repeat Step 2 until only the root node remains in the priority queue; this root node is the root of the completed Huffman tree.

2.3 Codestream-Based VQ Information Hiding Method

In 2013, Lee et al. proposed a codestream-based VQ information hiding method using correlations between neighboring blocks [12]. Some of the notation used by Lee et al. is presented in Table 1.

Table 1. Notation used by Lee et al. in the embedding and extraction phases of their codestream-based VQ information hiding method

Symbol	Definition
Y	The encoding index
YT	The top neighboring index of the encoding index
YL	The left neighboring index of the encoding index
fine_subcodebook1	Fine sub-codebook created by using the top neighboring index
fine_subcodebook0	Fine sub-codebook created by using the left neighboring index
coarse_subcodebook1	Coarse sub-codebook created by using the top neighboring index
coarse_subcodebook0	Coarse sub-codebook created by using the left neighboring index
cs	The size of a codebook
z	The half-length of a coarse sub-codebook
C_y	The C_y-th index in the corresponding coarse sub-codebook, where C_y is in the range 0 to $2z - 1$
C_{VQ}	The index table generated by the sorted codebook
w_1, w_2	The secret data to be hidden

In the embedding phase of Lee et al.'s method, a cover image is first divided into several non-overlapping blocks, then all blocks are encoded into a corresponding index via VQ encoding. Note that codewords in the codebook are sorted. Through this process, index table C_{VQ} is obtained, which can subsequently be used as a cover image within which the secret message may be embedded.

For each encoding index Y, four sub-codebooks (i.e., *fine_subcodebook1*, *fine_subcodebook0*, *coarse_subcodebook1*, and *coarse_subcodebook0*) are generated using rules below.

Table 2. The indicators and encoding rules of Lee et al.'s codestream-based VQ information hiding method [12]

Case	Indicator	Condition	Encode
1	00	If Y belongs to *fine_subcodebook0*	$00 \parallel w_1$
2	01	If Y belongs to *fine_subcodebook1*	$01 \parallel w_1$
3	100	If Y belongs to *coarse_subcodebook0*	$100 \parallel C_y \parallel w_2$
4	101	If Y belongs to *coarse_subcodebook1*	$101 \parallel C_y \parallel w_2$
5	11	None of the above	$11 \parallel Y$

(a) *fine_subcodebook1* $= \{YT\}$
(b) *fine_subcodebook0* $= \{YL\}$
(c) *coarse_subcodebook1* $= \{YT-z, \ldots, YT-1, YT+1, \ldots, YT+z\}$
(d) *coarse_subcodebook0* $= \{YL-z, \ldots, YL-1, YL+1, \ldots, YL+z\}$

If index Y is in *fine_subcodebook1* (i.e., index Y is the same as YT), the indicator is set to 01. If index Y is in *fine_subcodebook0* (i.e., index Y is the same as YL), the indicator is set to 00. If index Y is in *coarse_subcodebook0*, the indicator is set to 100 followed by index value C_y (in binary) of *coarse_subcodebook0*. If index Y is in *coarse_subcodebook1*, the indicator is set to 101 followed by index value C_y (in binary) of *coarse_subcodebook1*. Otherwise, the indicator is set to 11. Table 2 summarizes the indicators and the above encoding rules.

From Table 2, we observe that the indicator rule of Lee et al.'s method is fixed. For cases 1 and 2, the assumption is that occurrence rates are higher than for the other cases in the encoding. In recent years, the indicator rule of several codestream-based VQ information hiding methods have similarly been fixed; however, this fixed indicator approach may not be the best for all images. In this paper, we propose an elastic indicator model using Huffman coding for codestream-based VQ information methods. Our contributions here are not only solving the problem of the fixed indicator rule, but also enhancing security using a key. Details of our elastic indicator model are described in Sect. 3.

3   Our Proposed Elastic Indicator VQ Information Hiding Method

In this section, we present our elastic indicator VQ information hiding method that uses correlations of neighboring blocks. Our proposed method consists of four parts, i.e., encoding, decoding, variable selection, and encoding/decoding the key stream. In the initial encoding process, a cover image is translated into CVQ using the standard VQ compression algorithm. Next, we calculate the differences between neighboring blocks to further categorize results into different cases, details of which are discussed in Sect. 3.1. In the decoding process, the codestream is reconstructed in the form of a binary tree using a breadth-first traversal algorithm; the resulting binary tree is then used in the Huffman decoding process, details of which are presented in Sect. 3.2. To enhance security in the information hiding process, the sub-codebook generation policy, the number of sub-codebooks, the size of the sub-codebooks, and the Huffman code for different cases are all encoded as a key stream. Next, in Sect. 3.3, we introduce the variable selection and encoding/decoding key stream processes. To illustrate our proposed elastic indicator model, the symbols corresponding to our proposed model are defined in Table 3.

3.1   The Encoding Process

Generating $D_L(i, j)$, $D_T(i, j)$, and $D_A(i, j)$: The processing order of C_{VQ} starts with the first row, going from left to right, then moves to the first column, going from top to bottom, and finally the rest of the region, going from left to right and top to bottom. Here, $D_L(i, j)$, $D_T(i, j)$, and $D_A(i, j)$ are calculated using Eqs. (2a), (2b), and (2c), respectively. Thus, we have:

$$D_L(i, j) = C_{VQ}(i, j) - C_{VQ}(i, j - 1), \quad \text{if} \quad j \geq 2 \tag{2a}$$

$$D_T(i, j) = C_{VQ}(i, j) - C_{VQ}(i - 1, j), \quad \text{if} \quad i \geq 2 \tag{2b}$$

$$D_A(i, j) = \begin{cases} D_L(i, j), & \text{if } i = 1 \\ D_T(i, j), & \text{if } j = 1 \\ C_{VQ}(i, j) - \left\lfloor \frac{C_{VQ}(i-1,j) + C_{VQ}(i,j-1)}{2} \right\rfloor, & \text{if } i > 1 \text{ and } j > 1 \end{cases} \tag{2c}$$

Generating Sub-codebook SC_x and the Indicator: Figure 2 illustrates the concept of a sub-codebook. In the figure, each SC_x consists of a positive and negative part according to the distribution of D_A. Further, Ft_x indicates the middle position of each SC_x that is closest to zero, where the order of SC_x ranges from the minimum negative value to the maximum positive value. Equations to calculate Ft_x and SC_x are presented below as Eqs. (3) and (4), respectively. Note that not all difference values of D_A are in SC_x as it depends on the bits of each Z_x. We therefore have:

$$FT_x = \begin{cases} 1 & , \text{ if } x = 1 \\ FT_{x-1} + 2^{Z_{x-1}-1} & , \text{ otherwise} \end{cases} \tag{3}$$

$$SC_x = \begin{cases} [\{-2^{z_1-1} + ud\}, \{2^{z_1-1} - 1 + ud\}] & , \text{ if } x = 1 \\ [\{-FT_x - 2^{z_x-1} + 1 + ud\}, \{FT_x + 2^{z_x-1} - 2 + ud\}] - \sum_{k=1}^{x-1} SC_x & , \text{ otherwise} \end{cases} \tag{4}$$

Generating the *Ord*: Binary bits *Ord* are generated from D_A, Ft_x, and Z_x using Eq. (5) below. The output codestream Z_x-bit *Ord* in binary is generated from D_A and Ft_x in decimal. For the decoding process, the codestream

Table 3. Symbols for our proposed elastic indicator model

Symbol	Definition
i	The current processing index of the x-axis in the C_{VQ} table
j	The current processing index of y-axis in the C_{VQ} the table
x	The x-th sub-codebook, with a value between 1 and t
t	The number of sub-codebooks, with a value between 1 and 8
Z_x	The size of the x-th sub-codebook
p	The p-th element in a sub-codebook, with a value between 1 and 2^{Z_x}
n	The length of the secret message in bits
y	The y-th case, with a value between 1 and $t + 3$
$C_VQ(i, j)$	The index value of a VQ-compressed image in row i, column j
$cbsize$	The size of the codebook
$D_L(i, j)$	The difference between $C_{VQ}(i, j)$ and $C_{VQ}(i, j - 1)$, where $j > 1$
$D_T(i, j)$	The difference between $C_{VQ}(i, j)$ and $C_{VQ}(i - 1, j)$, where $i > 1$
$D_A(i, j)$	The difference between $C_{VQ}(i, j)$ and the average value of $D_L(i, j)$ and $D_T(i, j)$
$SC_{x,p}$	The p-th elements in the x-th sub-codebook
ud	The generating policy of SC_x, with a value of either 0 or 1; since D_A constructs part of SC_x, and D_A could be positive or negative, if $ud = 1$, a positive value starts at 1, whereas a negative value starts at 0; if $ud = 0$, a positive value starts at 0, while a negative value starts at -1
Ft_x	The middle position of the x-th sub-codebook; when $ud = 1$, $Ft_x = SC_{x,(p/2)} + 1$; when $ud = 0$, $Ft_x = SC_{x,(p/2)+1} - 1$
Hf_y	The Huffman code of the y-th case
$mod(k_1, k_2)$	The remainder of k_1 divided by k_2
$Bin2dec(k_3)$	The decimal value of k_3 bits
$Dec2bin(k_4, k_5)$	Conversion of decimal value k_4 to a bit stream of length k_5
E_{key}	The encoded key
E_{fin}	The encoded image
$\|$	The concatenation operator
$s_1...s_n$	The secret message bit stream of length n

is decoded and the order of the elements is decoded using Z_x-bit Ord first, thus recovering the original C_VQ. Thus, we have

$$
ord = \begin{cases}
Dec2bin(D_A + FT_x + 2^{Z_{x-1}} - 2, Z_x), & \text{if } ud = 1 \text{ and } D_A \leq 0 \\
Dec2bin(D_A - FT_x + 2^{Z_{x-1}} - 2, Z_x), & \text{if } ud = 1 \text{ and } D_A > 0 \\
Dec2bin(D_A + FT_x + 2^{Z_{x-1}} - 1, Z_x), & \text{if } ud = 0 \text{ and } D_A < 0 \\
Dec2bin(D_A - FT_x + 2^{Z_{x-1}} + 1, Z_x), & \text{otherwise}
\end{cases} \tag{5}
$$

Number of
value
in each SC

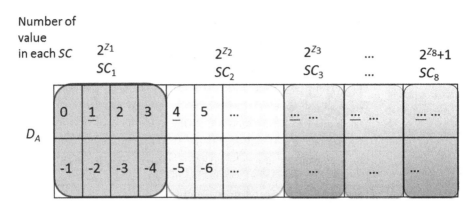

Fig. 2. Difference values of D_A in each SC, where $ud = 0$ and the underlined values denote Ft_x of SC_x

The Output Codestream of the Encoding Process. The output codestream of the encoding process consists of Huffman code Hf, Ord, and secret message s. The Huffman code is generated according to key and the frequency of each case, which we further discuss in Sect. 3.3. Table 4 presents the encoding rules for the codestream output. There are $t + 3$ cases in these encoding rules, where t denotes the number of sub-codebooks. If $D_L(i, j) = 0$ or $D_T(i, j) = 0$, the output codestream is encoded by indicator Hf_1 or Hf_2 and secret message $s_1...s_n$ (i.e., cases 1 and 2, respectively). If $D_A(i, j)$ is not in all SCs, the output codestream is encoded via $Hf_{t+3} \parallel C_{VQ}(i, j) \parallel s_1...s_n$ (i.e., case $t + 3$). In residual situations, the output codestream is encoded via $Hf_{k+2} \parallel ord \parallel s_1...s_n$ (i.e., case $k + 2$) according to $D_A(i, j)$ being in SC_k.

Table 4. The $t + 3$ encoding rules in our proposed method

Case	Condition	Encoding rule
1	$D_L = 0$	$Hf_1 \parallel s_1...s_n$
2	$D_T = 0$	$Hf_2 \parallel s_1...s_n$
3	$D_A \in SC_1$	$Hf_3 \parallel ord \parallel s_1...s_n$
4	$D_A \in SC_2$	$Hf_4 \parallel ord \parallel s_1...s_n$
$\cdots$		
$t + 1$	$D_A \in SC_{t-1}$	$Hf_{t+1} \parallel ord \parallel s_1...s_n$
$t + 2$	$D_A \in SC_t$	$Hf_{t+2} \parallel ord \parallel s_1...s_n$
$t + 3$	None of the above	$Hf_{t+3} \parallel C_{VQ}(i, j) \parallel s_1...s_n$

3.2   The Decoding Process

The decoding process is divided into two parts, i.e., decoding the key and the codestream. Before trying to decode the codestream, the key must first be decoded to construct the Huffman tree and retrieve t and Z_x. After the Huffman tree is reconstructed, the codestream can then be decoded according to the Huffman code represented by the given Huffman tree. The decoding algorithm is presented below.

Input: codestream, codebook, *key*
Output: secret message s, cover VQ image
Step 1: retrieve t, Z_x, and the Huffman tree from key (see Sect. 3.3.1) and generate Ft_1 to Ft_t using Eq. (3)
Step 2: set case $t+4$ as the root of the Huffman tree
Step 3: create an empty C_{VQ} table
Step 4: read $log_2(cbsize)$ bits as the first node and set to $C_{VQ}(1,1)$
Step 5: retrieve the C_{VQ} table and secret message s from the Huffman tree
switch(node)
{
    Case (0):
        Read one bit, a, for the codestream; if bit a is 0, move to the left child; otherwise (i.e., if a $= 1$), move to the right child
    Case (1):
        Set $C_{VQ}(i,j) = C_{VQ}(i,j-1)$, read n bits as the secret message, then return to the root
    Case (2):
        Set $C_{VQ}(i,j) = C_{VQ}(i-1,j)$, read n bits as the secret message, then return to the root
    Case ($3 \sim t+2$):
        Read Z_{node-2} bits and calculate $C_{VQ}(i,j)$ using Eq. (6), read n bits as the secret message, then return to the root
    Case ($t+3$):
        Read $log_2(cbsize)$ bits and set to $C_{VQ}(i,j)$, read n bits as the secret message, then return to the root
    Case ($t+4$):
        if j is less than the width of C_{VQ}, then $j = j+1$;
        else if i is less than the height of C_{VQ}, then $i = i+1$ and $j = 1$;
        else $C_{VQ}(i,j)$ is reconstructed and secret message s is decoded
}

$$C_{VQ}(i,j-1) = \begin{cases} g + Bin2dec(Z_x) - Ft_x - 2^{Z_x-1} + 1 + ud, & \text{if } Bin2dec(Z_x) < 2^{Z_x-1} \\ g + Bin2dec(Z_x) - Ft_x - 2^{Z_x-1} - 1 + ud, & \text{otherwise} \end{cases},$$

$$\text{where } g = \begin{cases} C_{VQ}(i,j-1), & \text{if } i = 1 \\ C_{VQ}(i-1,j), & \text{if } j = 1 \\ \left\lfloor \frac{C_{VQ}(i,j-1)+C_{VQ}(i-1,j)}{2} \right\rfloor, & \text{if } j \geq 2 \text{ and } j \geq 2 \end{cases}$$

$$(6)$$

Step 6: use the VQ algorithm with the codebook to recover the image

Generating SC_s and the Huffman Tree: When receiving the codestream, the SC_s generation process is the same as the encoding process described in Eq. (4) above. The difference here is that the Huffman tree acquired by decoding key does not have to be translated into the Huffman code; instead, we assign indicators to each node and assign case $t + 4$ as the root.

The Purpose of Assigning Value to Each Node and the Decoding Process: When decoding an image, each node can be seen as a case that can be used to recover original $C_{VQ}(i, j)$. To begin decoding, we first read a bit stream of length $log_2(cbsize)$, assigning the value to the top left corner as $C_{VQ}(1, 1)$. Next, we construct the Huffman tree, where different cases lead to different processes.

3.3   Variable Selections and the Encoding/Decoding Process of *key*

In our proposed elastic indicator VQ information hiding method, we use key to record variables used for the encoding and decoding processes. The key provides variety for the encoding/decoding process, thus enhancing security. The first step in our proposed method is to find a suitable variable combination, then encode the selected parameters into the key, which must be shared between sender and receiver. In this subsection, we discuss two key parts of this process, i.e., the encoding procedure, which is presented in Sect. 3.3.1, and the decoding procedure, which is presented in Sect. 3.3.2.

3.3.1   The Encoding Procedure of Keystream *key*

After finding SC_x and the indicators, the input variables, including ud, t, Z_x, and Huffman tree T, must be encoded into keystream *key*. The input variables can then be further used in the C_{VQ} encoding/decoding process. Since Ft_x can be obtained via Eq. (3), it does not have to be included in keystream *key*. The processing order of keystream *key* is first the input variables, then the Huffman tree of indicators.

A. Transforming Variables ud, t, and Z_x: Since ud can be only zero or one, one bit is sufficient to store ud; similarly, t is between one and eight, thus three bits are sufficient for storing the information (i.e., $t - 1$). Because Z_x represents the length of bits of SC_x, and the value of SC_x must be between one and $cbsize$, the value of Z_x must between one and $log_2(cbsize) - 1$. To save space, Z_x is re-encoded and combined with $Ekey$ using Eq. (7) as follows:

$$E_{key} = E_{key} \parallel Dec2bin(\sum_{x=1}^{t}(Z_x - 1) \times ((log_2cbsize) - 1)^{t-x}, \lceil log_2((log_2cbsize) - 1)^t\rceil) \ (7)$$

B. Translating the Huffman Tree of Indicators: After the input variables are encoded, the indicators are encoded using the translation process for indicators. Since indicators are stored in a binary tree, the entire structure must be encoded into keystream *key*. According to the properties of a Huffman tree, the number of children of each node is either zero or two. Therefore, all cases of our proposed encoding method are stored in the leaves of the Huffman tree, thus we have $t + 3$ leaves and $2t + 5$ nodes overall. Assume that each node requires ns bits to be stored. We use t as a boundary, i.e., if $t > 4$, then $ns = 4$, otherwise

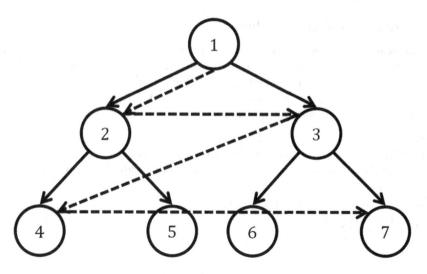

Fig. 3. The order we use to scan all nodes as part of translating the Huffman tree.

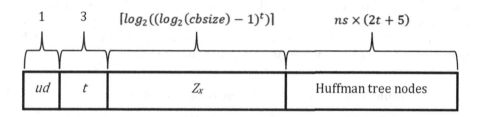

Fig. 4. The format of keystream key in our proposed method.

if $t \leq 4$, then $ns = 3$. During the translation procedure, we use a breadth-first traversal algorithm such that each node is translated into a binary bit stream of length ns, as illustrated in Fig. 3. Since the leaves have already been assigned an index based on which case they fall into, we assign zero to non-leaf nodes. The format of keystream key is illustrated in Fig. 4.

C. The key-encoding algorithm

Input: ud, t, Z, Huffman tree
Output: E_{key}
Step 1: $E_{key} = $ null and output 1-bit ud to E_{key}
Step 2: output 3-bit $(t - 1)$ to E_{key}
Step 3: use Eq. (7) to re-encode Z_x as $\lceil log_2((log_2(cbsize) - 1)^t) \rceil$-bit and output the result to E_{key}
Step 4: output all tree $2t + 5$ nodes as $ns \times (2t + 5)$ bits to E_{key} by a breadth-first traversal algorithm

3.3.2   Key-Decoding Procedure

A. Recovering Three Variables ud, t, and Z_x of SC_x: Before the decoding procedure, ud must be decoded from the first bit of codestream E_{key}. Next, the following three bits are decoded as t, which indicates the number of sub-codebooks. Finally, Z_x is recovered from the next $\lceil log_2((log_2(cbsize) - 1)^t) \rceil$ bits. This algorithm is summarized below.

Step 1: Fetch 1 bit from E_{key} as ud
Step 2: Fetch 3 bits from residual E_{key} and plus 1 as t
Step 3: Fetch $\lceil log_2((log_2(cbsize) - 1)^t) \rceil$ bits from residual E_{key} as follows
for $i = 1$ to $t - 1$
$\quad Z_{t-i+1} = mod(z_k, log_2(cbsize) - 1) + 1$
$\quad Z_k = \left\lfloor \frac{zk}{log_2(cbsize)-1} \right\rfloor$
end for
$Z_1 = zk + 1$

B. Reconstructing the Huffman Tree:
During the reconstruction process, the leftmost node of each layer is recorded in the *pointtable* table. As shown in Fig. 5, the data structure of the tree node consists of a value and three pointers, which point to the left child, right child, and right sibling. Other symbols are defined as shown in Table 5.

Table 5. Symbols used for reconstructing the Huffman tree

Symbol	Definition
null	Null pointer, indicating the end of a link
$point_1$	A pointer that points to the parent node of the node to be retrieved
$point_2$	A pointer that points to the node to be retrieved
$pointtable(g)$	The leftmost node of layer g
$node(q)$	The q-th recovered node, with q between 1 and $2t + 5$

The Huffman tree is reconstructed after Z_x is decoded. There are $2t + 3$ nodes in the Huffman tree. The algorithm below illustrates the process of reconstructing a Huffman tree, with variable temp indicating the node currently being processed.

Step 1: Initial process
$\quad$**Set** temp = node(1)
$\quad$Create the *pointtable* table and initialize *pointtable*(1)=temp
$\quad$**Set** the right sibling of temp = null
$\quad$**Set** $point_1$ = temp
$\quad$**Set** root = temp
$\quad$**Set** temp = node(2)

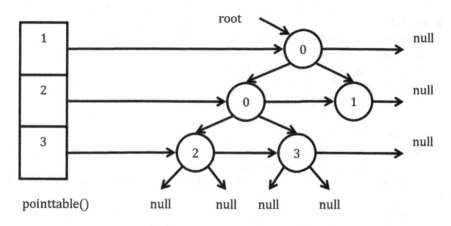

Fig. 5. Illustrating the structure for reconstructing the Huffman tree.

Set the left child of $point_1=$ temp
Set $point_2=$ temp
Set pointtable(2) $=$ temp
Step 2: Find the position of the reconstructed node
    while $point_1$ is not zero or $point_1$ is zero but the right child of $point_1$ is not null
    do
        if the right sibling of $point_1$ is not null, **then**
            Set $point_1$ to the right sibling of $point_1$
        else
            Set the right sibling of $point_2=$ null
            Set $point_2$ to the next layer of $point_2$ in $pointtable$
            Set $point_1$ to the right sibling of the next layer of $point_1$ in $pointtable$
Step 3: Reconstruct the node
Step 4: Check that all nodes are reconstructed
    Repeat **Step** 2 and **Step** 3 until there are no more $node(q)$ instances

C. Key-Decoding Algorithm
Input: E_{key}
Output: ud, t, Z_1 Z_t, Huffman tree (indicator)
Step 1: Retrieve ud
    $ud =$ the first bit of E_key
Step 2: Retrieve t
    $t =$ the second bit to fourth bit of $E_key + 1$
Step 3: Retrieve Z
    Retrieve $\lceil log_2((log_2(cbsize) - 1)^t) \rceil$ bits, and calculate Z_x using the approach described in Sect. 3.3.2.1 **Step 4**   Each node in ns-bit is decided by t and retrieves the ns-bit as the node for the steps that follow:

Step 4.1

    Create *pointtable* and initialize as *pointtable*(1) = root

    Set the right sibling of root = null

    Set the value of root = *node*(1)

    Set *pointtable*(2) = *node*(2)

    Set the left child of root = *node*(2)

    Set $point_1$ = root

    Set $point_2$ = *node*(2)

Step 4.2

    for the remaining *node*() instances:

        while $point_1$ is not 0 or $point_1$ is 0 but the right child of $point_1$ is not null:

        do{

            if the right sibling of $point_1$ is not null, then

                Set $point_1$ to the right sibling of $point_1$

            else

                Set the right sibling of $point_2$ = null

                Set $point_2$ to the next layer of $point_2$ in *pointtable*

                Set $point_1$ to the right sibling of the next layer of $point_1$ in *pointtable*

        }

        Set temp = *node*(q)

        if the left child of $point_1$ is null, **then**

            Set temp = the left child of $point_1$

        else

            Set temp = the right child of $point_1$

            Set the right sibling of $point_2$ = temp

            Set temp = $point_2$

    End for

4   Experimental Results

In this section, we present some of our experimental results in which we compare our proposed method and Lee et al.'s method. With a codebook 128, we used 10 test images, as shown in Fig. 6. All test images were grayscale images with uniform sizes of 512×512. Our experimental results relate to three aspects, i.e., compression, security, and speed. More details are provided in the subsections that follow.

Further, we used pure bit rate (PBR) as the performance measurement, which is defined as shown below. We used PBR to show the compression capability of an algorithm, where the smaller PBR values, the better the performance. PBR is defined as

$$PBR = \frac{\text{the outputted codestream}}{M \times N},$$

where M and N denote the width and height of the test image, respectively.

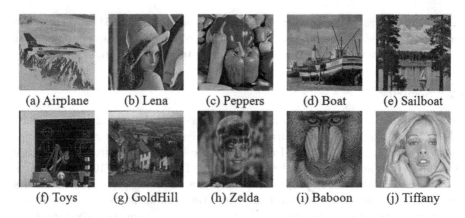

(a) Airplane   (b) Lena   (c) Peppers   (d) Boat   (e) Sailboat

(f) Toys   (g) GoldHill   (h) Zelda   (i) Baboon   (j) Tiffany

Fig. 6. The 10 grayscale test images that we used in our experiments.

4.1 Compression

Table 6 shows PBR values for our proposed method and Lee et al.'s scheme using various test images and a codebook with 128 codeword. According to these results, when compared to Lee et al.'s method, our proposed scheme produced better PBR in all circumstances. The average PBR value of the proposed method is lower than Lee et al.'s scheme, especially in the two images (Baboon and Tiffany), the performance is much better than Lee et al.'s scheme. Considering the capacity of compression, the result of using the Tiffany image as a cover

Table 6. PBR comparisons between our proposed method and Lee et al.'s scheme with $cbsize = 128$ [12]

In bit	Proposed method				Lee et al.'s scheme	
	codestream (A)	key stream (B)	(A) + (B)	PBR	codestream	PBR
	cbsize = 256				z = 8	
Airplane	58047	77	58124	0.222	62803	0.240
Lena	65662	109	65771	0.251	72031	0.275
Peppers	64456	109	64565	0.246	70514	0.269
Boat	61109	77	61186	0.233	65248	0.249
Sailboat	67317	45	67362	0.257	71178	0.272
Toys	39015	54	39069	0.149	47876	0.183
Gold Hill	73974	109	74083	0.283	79586	0.304
Zelda	68748	109	68857	0.263	76675	0.292
Baboon	99940	109	100049	0.382	109028	0.416
Tiffany	35619	109	35728	0.136	46851	0.179
Average	63389	91	63479	0.242	70179	0.268

image with cbsize $= 128$ and $z = 4$ produced a $35{,}728/46{,}851 = 0.762$ ratio versus that of Lee et al.'s scheme. From the above key results, we conclude that our proposed scheme has better performance in terms of compression.

4.2   Security

Since the underlying process of our proposed scheme is largely affected by variable SC_x and the indicator, we used a greedy algorithm to find a suitable combination of SC_x and indicator by counting the number and size of each case to estimate the size of the final coding result. Then, the top 1000 candidates were selected for use in our proposed method. Based on the experimental results presented in Table 7, compression ratios were very similar across all of the cases, thus we decided to use a randomly selected candidate in our proposed method.

Table 7. PBR values for different candidates in our proposed method

Bits of encoded image PBR	Minimum	250-th	500-th	750-th	1000-th	Difference between the minimum and the 1000-th
Airplane	58124	58274	58317	58343	58364	240
	0.222	0.222	0.222	0.223	0.223	0.00092
Lena	65771	65980	66019	66047	66068	297
	0.251	0.252	0.252	0.252	0.252	0.00113
Peppers	64565	64700	64739	64765	64790	225
	0.246	0.247	0.247	0.247	0.247	0.00086
Boat	61186	61291	61341	61379	61401	215
	0.233	0.234	0.234	0.234	0.234	0.00082
Sailboat	67362	67498	67577	67624	67648	286
	0.257	0.257	0.258	0.258	0.258	0.00109
Toys	39069	39178	39222	39244	39261	192
	0.149	0.149	0.150	0.150	0.150	0.00073
Gold Hill	74083	74305	74379	74433	74474	391
	0.283	0.283	0.284	0.284	0.284	0.00149
Zelda	68857	69048	69118	69159	69211	354
	0.263	0.263	0.264	0.264	0.264	0.00135
Baboon	100049	100344	100450	100545	100605	556
	0.382	0.383	0.383	0.384	0.384	0.00212
Tiffany	35728	35802	35836	35877	35910	182
	0.136	0.137	0.137	0.137	0.137	0.00069

5   Conclusions

In this paper, we proposed an information hiding method based on VQ compression that also incorporated neighboring correlation and an elastic indictor. In our proposed method, indices are encoded according to difference values from adjacent indices, and elastic sub-codebooks are used to improve the compression rate. Further, we demonstrated three steps for speeding up execution times. Our experimental results confirmed the effectiveness of our proposed elastic VQ information hiding method. In terms of embedding capacity and compression rate, experimental results showed that performance of our proposed method was better than Lee et al.'s method [12]. Even with the additional key stream, by using our approach, compression rates can be reduced by approximately 10% on average.

Acknowledgments. This research was partially supported by the Ministry of Science and Technology of the Republic of China under the Grant MOST 104-2221-E-015-001-, MOST 105-2221-E-015-002-, and the Oriental Institute of Technology under the Grant RD1050025 and 151001-708.

References

1. Dadgostar, H., Afsari, F.: Image steganography based on interval-valued intuitionistic fuzzy edge detection and modified LSB. J. Inf. Secur. Appl. **30**, 94–104 (2016)
2. Lerch-Hostalot, D., Megías, D.: LSB matching steganalysis based on patterns of pixel differences and random embedding. Comput. Secur. **32**, 192–206 (2013)
3. Govind, P.V.S., Sajila, M.K., Varghese, B.M.: A two stage data hiding scheme with high capacity based on interpolation and difference expansion. Procedia Technol. **24**, 1311–1316 (2016)
4. Shiu, C.W., Chen, Y.C., Hong, W.: Encrypted image-based reversible data hiding with public key cryptography from difference expansion. Signal Process. Image Commun. **39**, 226–233 (2015)
5. Ou, B., Li, X., Zhao, Y., Ni, R., Shi, Y.Q.: Pairwise prediction-error expansion for efficient reversible data hiding. IEEE Trans. Image Process. **22**, 5010–5021 (2013)
6. Li, X., Zhang, W., Gui, X., Yang, B.: Efficient reversible data hiding based on multiple histograms modification. IEEE Trans. Inf. Forensics Secur. **10**, 2016–2027 (2015)
7. Rad, R.M., Wong, K., Guo, J.M.: Reversible data hiding by adaptive group modification on histogram of prediction errors. Signal Process. **125**, 315–328 (2016)
8. Lin, Y.K.: A data hiding scheme based upon DCT coefficient modification. Comput. Stand. Interfaces **36**, 855–862 (2014)
9. Chang, P.C., Chung, K.L., Chen, J.J., Lin, C.H., Lin, T.J.: A DCT/DST-based error propagation-free data hiding algorithm for HEVC intra-coded frames. J. Vis. Commun. Image Represent. **25**, 239–253 (2014)
10. Mao, J.F., Niu, X.X., Xiao, G., Sheng, W.G., Zhang, N.N.: A steganalysis method in the DCT domain. Multimed. Tools Appl. **75**, 5999–6019 (2016)
11. Phadikar, A., Maity, S.P., Mandal, M.: Novel wavelet-based QIM data hiding technique for tamper detection and correction of digital images. J. Vis. Commun. Image Represent. **23**, 454–466 (2012)

12. Lee, J.D., Chiou, Y.H., Guo, J.M.: Lossless data hiding for VQ indices based on neighboring correlation. Inf. Sci. **221**, 419–438 (2013)
13. Qin, C., Hu, Y.C.: Reversible data hiding in VQ index table with lossless coding and adaptive switching mechanism. Signal Process. **129**, 48–55 (2016)
14. Lin, C.C., Liu, X.L., Yuan, S.M.: Reversible data hiding for VQ-compressed images based on search-order coding and state-codebook mapping. Inf. Sci. **293**, 314–326 (2015)
15. Linde, Y., Buzo, A., Gray, R.M.: An algorithm for vector quantizer design. IEEE Trans. Commun. **28**, 84–95 (1980)
16. Huffman, D.A.: A method for the construction of minimum-redundancy codes. Proc. IRE **40**, 1098–1101 (1952)

Idology and Its Applications in Public Security and Network Security

Shenghui Su[1,3(✉)], Jianhua Zheng[2], Shuwang Lü[2,5], Zhiqiu Huang[3],
Zhoujun Li[4], and Zhenmin Tang[1]

[1] Security Innovation Center, Nanjing University of Science and Technology,
Nanjing 210094, People's Republic of China
reesse@126.com
[2] Laboratory of Information Security,
University of Chinese Academy of Sciences,
Beijing 100039, People's Republic of China
[3] College of Computers,
Nanjing University of Aeronautics and Astronautics,
Nanjing 211106, People's Republic of China
[4] School of Computers, Beihang University, Beijing 100191
People's Republic of China
[5] Laboratory of Computational Complexity,
BFID Corporation, Beijing 100098, People's Republic of China

Abstract. Fraud (swindling money, property, or authority by fictionizing, counterfeiting, forging, or imitating things, or by feigning persons privately) forms its threats against public security and network security. Anti-fraud is essentially the identification of a person or thing. In this paper, the authors first propose the concept of idology - a systematic and scientific study of identifications of persons and things, and give the definitions of a symmetric identity and an asymmetric identity. Discuss the converting symmetric identities (e.g., fingerprints) to asymmetric identities. Make a comparison between a symmetric identity and an asymmetric identity, and emphasize that symmetric identities cannot guard against inside jobs. Compare asymmetric RFIDs with BFIDs, and point out that a BFID is lightweight, economical, convenient, and environmentalistic, and more suitable for the anti-counterfeit and source tracing of consumable merchandise such as food, drugs, and cosmetics. The authors design the structure of a united verification platform for BFIDs and the composition of an identification system, and discuss the wide applications of BFIDs in public security and network security - antiterrorism and dynamic passwords for example.

Keywords: Idology · Symmetric identity · Asymmetric identity · Identification · Anti-fraud · Digital signature · Hash function · United verification platform

This work is supported by MOST with Project 2007CB311100 and 2009AA01Z441.

G.A. Wang et al. (Eds.): PAISI 2017, LNCS 10241, pp. 129–149, 2017.
DOI: 10.1007/978-3-319-57463-9_9

1 Introduction

Fraud (swindling money, property, or authority by fictionizing, counterfeiting, forging, or imitating things, or by feigning other persons in private) exists ubiquitously in both the physical world and the digital world (cyberspace). It is age-old but active, and prohibited by laws but not prevented efficiently with techniques.

Fraud forms its threat against public securities. For instance, counterfeit of merchandise brands (especially food and drugs) [1, 2], forgery of papery diplomas or certificates [3], forgery of financial bills or notes [4], fiction of financial accounts [5], etc.

Fraud forms its threat against network securities. For instance, fiction of IP addresses, juggle of IP addresses [6], non-license of programs (note that the execution of malicious program is ascribed to non-license) [7], non-authorization of websites (namely fishing websites) [8], forgery of electronic documents [9], wiretapping of user passwords [10], etc.

Fraud is different from secret-outing. Keeping of secret relies on the application of encryption technology while prevention of fraud relies on the improvement and application of identification technology. Sometimes, symmetric ciphers are used for authentication, but it is not strict identification, and only the re-meeting between two friends who hold the same private key.

Throughout this paper, unless otherwise specified, the sign % means "modulo", $\overline{M}$ means "$M - 1$" with M prime, $\lg x$ denotes the logarithm of x to the base 2, $\neg b_i$ does the opposite value of a bit b_i, $\not{p}$ does the maximal prime allowed in a coprime sequence, $|x|$ does the absolute value of a number x, $\|x\|$ does the order of an element $x \% M$, $|S|$ does the size of a set S, and $\gcd(a, b)$ represents the greatest common divisor of two integers. Without ambiguity, "$\% M$" is usually omitted in expressions.

2 Several Definitions Relevant to Identification

In terms of american dictionaries, an identity is said to be *the set of characteristics* by which a person or thing is definitively recognizable or known, *the awareness* that an individual or group has of being a distinct and persisting entity, *the condition* of being a certain person or thing, *information* such as an identification number used to establish or prove a person's individuality [11], or *the set* of behavioral or personal characteristics by which an individual is recognizable as a member of a group [12]. Therefore, the identity concept is not only applicable to a person, but also a thing such as a material article, a machine, an organization, etc.

2.1 Identity, Subject, Object, and Idology

An identity referred here is not the social attribute of a person or thing — a nobleman or commoner, a luxury or pedlary for example, but the natural attribute of a person or thing, relating to inherence — the head portrait or fingerprint of a person stored in the chip of a passport for example.

Definition 1. An identity is a congenital mark of a person or thing (including organization) by which the nativity, derivation, affiliation, or/and distinctiveness of the person or thing are determined.

Definition 2. The administration of persons, the registry of users or organizations, the producer, maker, issuer, or approver of things is called a subject, and a person or thing is called an object.

Two affairs, namely the prevention of secret-outing and prevention of fraud, occurred simultaneously along with human beings wars, which indicates that identification technology is the same archaic as encryption technology. For example, in 257 B.C. belonging the Warring States Period of China, a son of the king of Wei State whose feoff was in XinLing rescued Zhao State successfully by stealing the half BingFu, dispatching the troop, reenforcing Handan, and defeating the enemy from Qin State [13].

A BingFu is a commander's tally which convinces the chief general at a military base that an order to maneuver troops comes indeed from the king or emperor of a state or nation, and is split into two halves — the right reserved by the king or emperor and the left given to the chief general (Fig. 1).

Fig. 1. A BingFu — the identity of military orders of the first emperor of Qin Dynasty

In Fig. 1, the right and left of the BingFu have the same inscriptions: This is a tally for maneuvering soldiers in armour, the right is reserved by the emperor, and the left is given to the chief general at YangLing.

Notice that the inscriptions of the right and left are arranged *asymmetrically*. When the first emperor maneuvers troops, the right must coincide with the left (Fig. 2).

Definition 3. Idology is a systematic and scientific study of identity confection, identity denotation, identity sensing, and identity verification for the identification of a person or thing.

Identity confection is to say to make the characteristics of a subject and/or the characteristics of an object into an identity which is a string, graph, or cast.

Identity denotation is to say to set the identity of an object into a place which is a part of the object, or bound with the object.

Identity sensing is to say to detect (or perceive) an identity manually or automatically, extract the identity essence, and send (or transmit) it to a verification platform.

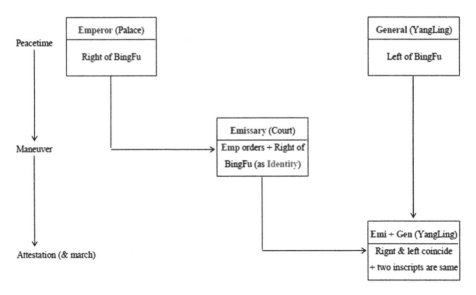

Fig. 2. Process of maneuvering troops with a BingFu

Identity verification is to say to affirm the correctness or facticity of an identity by evidence and logic, and on occasion return the result and related information to an inquirer [14].

As a branch of knowledge or teaching, idology has its research purpose, theoretical foundation, and exploration field.

The research purpose of idology is to prevent fraud in both the physical world and the digital world.

The theoretical foundation of idology involves computational complexity, informatics, number theory, abstract algebra, the design and analysis of algorithms, data structure, hash function, digital signature, security proof theory, etc.

The exploration field of idology includes symmetric identities, asymmetric identities, isomeric identities, communication networks, internet of things, big data, cloud computing, pattern recognition, biometrics, electronic or imaging sensors, software engineering, etc.

2.2 Symmetric Identity and Asymmetric Identity

On the view of practice, identities present symmetric and asymmetric modalities.

2.2.1 Symmetric Identities

Definition 4. A graph or a string which is verified through direct comparison or simply computational comparison with a duplicate stored in advance is called a symmetric identity.

The evolution of symmetric identities experiences two phases.

- Classical Symmetric Identities
  They include passwords or watchwords which emerged first within the ancient Roman military [15], stamps (equivalent to handwritten signatures) which occurred at least two thousand years ago — the Nephrite Stamp of the Empress in the Western Han Dynasty for example [16], watermarks of which the idea was first brought forward by an Italian in 1282 [17], trademarks which are thought of as being used first by blacksmiths of the Roman Empire period from 27 BC to 476 AD [18], etc.
- Modern Symmetric Identities
  They include holographic labels which occurred in the late 1970's (Left of Fig. 3) [19], electronic query/supervision codes which emerged in the early 1990's [20], quick response codes (namely two-dimensional codes) which occurred in 1994 (Right of Fig. 3) [21], etc.

Fig. 3. A holographic label and QR code

Especially, it should be pointed out that human biological characteristics such as a fingerprint and iris (Fig. 4) [22] are also a type of symmetric identity, where a fingerprint was applied to biometric authentication and criminalistics in the early 20th century [23, 24].

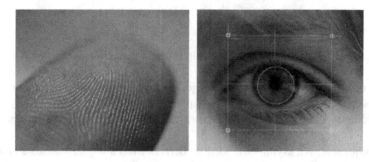

Fig. 4. A fingerprint and iris

Among the above symmetric identities, a watermark, trademark, and holographic label are collective identities of which each is assigned the same kind of object, a two-dimensional code, electronic supervision code, fingerprint, and iris are individual identities, and a stamp and password may be either collective identities or individual identities.

Note that because the symmetric identities are easily copied, imitated, forged, or liable to being manipulated by an inside jobber, they are insecure sometimes [25].

2.2.2   Asymmetric Identities

Definition 5. A cast or a string which is verified through the matching the left half with the right half or the public key with the private key is called an asymmetric identity [26].

The evolution of asymmetric identities also experiences two phases.

- Classical Asymmetric Identity
  It is only a BingFu (namely a commander's tally) which is separated into two asymmetric halves, and appeared in China at least two thousand and two hundred years ago (Figs. 1 and 2) [13].
- Modern Asymmetric Identities
  They include a RFID (Radio Frequency IDentity) which is embedded with a chip, occurred roughly in 1983 [27], and adopted digital signatures for anti-counterfeit in the late 1990's (Fig. 5) [28, 29], and a BFID (BingFu Identity Digitized) which is without a chip, originated from the early 2012's (Fig. 6) [30], and is composed of 16–22 printable characters corresponding to a digital signature.

Fig. 5. A RFID with a chip storing a digital signature

From now on, an asymmetric identity just indicates a modern asymmetric identity for a classical asymmetric identity is not applied any longer.

According to Definition 5, an asymmetric identity has the following four properties [26]:

① Uniqueness: An asymmetric identity derives from a digital signature hiding the distinctive information of an object and being actually different from one another. Thus, it can uniquely represent one object in a domain.

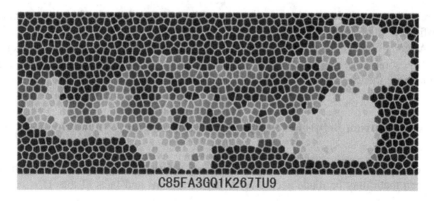

Fig. 6. A BFID consisting of 80 bits equivalent to 16 characters

② Anti-forgery: An asymmetric identity is obtained through a digital signing algorithm. Only can a specific public key which corresponds to the private key of a subject check it, and other public keys cannot check it. Consequently, the sufficiency of anti-forgery can be ensured.

③ Hiddenness: An asymmetric identity contains obscurely the characteristic of an object — a serial number, scaled time, biological attribute for example, and the private key of a subject.

④ Asymmetry: An asymmetric identity is confected with a private key, verified with a public key, and different from a symmetric identity which has no key or only one key.

Summarily, an asymmetric identity may produce important effects on authentication, anti-forgery, source tracing, and distribution monitoring.

Definition 6. An asymmetric identity which consists of only 16–22 characters, and does not need to be stored in a chip is called a lightweight asymmetric identity.

Because an asymmetric identity confected through the optimized REESSE1 +signing scheme may be 16–22 characters long (see Sect. 3.1), it is lightweight in terms of Definition 6 [26]. A lightweight asymmetric identity is also called a BFID.

2.2.3   Conversion of a Symmetric Identity to an Asymmetric Identity

In remote service mode based on the Internet, the employment of a symmetric identity is probably insecure. We analyze an affair that a fingerprint as a password is used to log on a remote e-mail server. Under the circumstances, there exist two security risks:

① a fingerprint template stored in the server may be acquired by inside unauthorized technicians;

② a fingerprint instance transmitted on the Internet may be wiretapped by deliberate eavesdroppers on logon.

Therefore, when a symmetric identity such as a fingerprint or string password is used remotely, it needs to be converted into an asymmetric identity through a hash function and a lightweight digital signing algorithm by the owner of a fingerprint or a secret string who holds a private key and a public key. The latter is placed on a united verification platform or a server.

Although any digitized symmetric identity may be converted into an asymmetric identity, sometimes the mixed or combined utilization of a symmetric identity and an asymmetric identity is needed.

2.3   Comparison Between a Symmetric Identity and an Asymmetric Identity

A symmetric identity and an asymmetric identity act as different roles. A comparison between them may be made according to the definitions and facts (Table 1).

Table 1. A comparison between a sym. identity and an asym. identity

	Attesting method	Bearing character of an object	Inside job	United attestation	Anti-forgery	Source tracing	Internet of things based on clouds
Sym. ID	Symmetric	No	Possible	Infeasible	No	No	Infeasible
Asym. ID	Asymmetric	Yes	Impossible	Feasible	Yes	Yes	Feasible

It is well known that a symmetric identity such as an official stamp or electronic supervision code is easily imitated through an inside job or outside job since it does not bear the characteristic of an object [31]. It follows that an official stamp or electronic supervision code attached to authority is usually considered as trustworthy, but not secure. Note that trustworthiness does not equal security.

We can understand from Table 1 that the two primary advantages of an asymmetric identity are the prevention of inside jobs and the realizability of a united verification platform.

Asymmetric identities do not repulse symmetric identities. On some occasions, they are employed miscellaneously.

2.4   Comparison Between a Symmetric Identity and an Asymmetric Identity

A RFID may be used for the anti-counterfeit of a merchant article, and similarly, a BFID may be used for the anti-counterfeit of a merchant article, especially a consumable commodity. Why is a BFID brought in yet? This needs to make a comparison between them (Table 2).

Note that there is 16 = 80/5, namely a character is twice-hexadecimal.

Table 2. A comparison between a RFID and a BFID

	Security	Basic algorithm	Character-length	Storage	Sensing	Cost	Con-venience	Environ-mentalism
RFID	$2 \wedge 80$	ECC\160 or RSA\1024	48 or 204	Chip	Radio frequency	High	Low	Weak
BFID	$2 \wedge 80$	REESSE1+\80	16	Scrip or others	Light ray or others	Low	High	Strong

It can be understanded from Table 2 that a BFID is tightly pertinent to a new specific algorithm, lightweight, economical, green, and easy to use (no need of card readers — for example).

3 Foundation of Lightweight Asymmetric Identities

A digital signature in a RFID chip is generally produced with the ECC or RSA signing scheme [32–34] while a digital signature corresponding to a BFID is produced with the optimized REESSE1+ signing scheme [35, 36]. It is well known that a digital signing scheme is devised on the basis of intractable computational problems which are primarily constructed on the subbasis of computational complexity theory [37, 38].

Concretely speaking, the security of ECC is based on an elliptic curve discrete logarithm problem (ECDLP) [33, 39], the security of RSA is based on an integer factorization problem (IFP) [34, 40], and the security of REESSE1+ , including a hash function resistant to birthday attack [41], is based on the three new hardnesses and one classical hardness: a multivariate permutation problem (MPP), an anomalous subset product problem (ASPP), a transcendental logarithm problem (TLP) [35, 42], and a polynomial root finding problem (PRFP) which is equivalent to the fact that a polynomial of high degree has only exponential time solutions at present [43, 44]. Similar to PRFP, the hardnesses MPP, ASPP, and TLP have no subexponential time solutions so far [36, 42].

3.1 Optimized REESSE1+ Signing Scheme

The optimized REESSE1+ digital signing scheme includes three algorithms for key-pair generation, digital signing, and signature authentication.

A digital signature is the output of the digital signing algorithm which takes a private key and an information digest as input [35].

The length of an optimized REESSE1+ modulus may only be 80 bits under the security of magnitude $2 \wedge 80$ while the length of an ECC modulus is 160 bits under the same security. The length of an optimized REESSE1+ signature only is 160 bits while the length of a ECC signature is at least 320 bits under the same security [33, 35].

3.1.1   Key Generation Algorithm

Assume that $đ, Đ, T, S$ are pairwise coprime integers, where $đ \in [5, 2^8]$, $T \geq 2^9$, $Đ \geq 2^{54}$ containing a prime $\geq 2^{52}$, and $\lceil \lg(đ\,Đ T) \rceil \geq 64$.

> INPUT: a modulus length m with $80 \leq m \leq 96$;
>   a sequence length n with $80 \leq n \leq m \leq 96$;
>   a set $\Lambda = \{2, 3, \ldots, 863\}$.
> S1: Produce appropriate parameters $đ, Đ, T$.
>   Produce the first $n/2$ natural primes $p_1, \ldots, p_{n/2}$.
>   Randomly produce a coprime sequence $\{A_1, \ldots, A_n\}$ with $A_i \in \Lambda$.
>   Randomly produce a set $\Omega = \{+/-5, +/-7, \ldots, +/-(2n+3)\}$,
>   where every sign $+/-$ means that "$+$" or "$-$" is selected.
> S2: Find a prime M making $\lceil \lg M \rceil = m$, $(đ\,Đ T) \mid \overline{M}$ and $\prod_{i=1}^{k} p_i^{e_i} \mid \overline{M}$,
>   where k, e_i and p_k meet $\prod_{i=1}^{k} e_i \approx 2^8$ and $p_k < p_{n/2}$.
>   Pick $S \in (1, \overline{M})$ making $\gcd(S, \overline{M}) = 1$ and $S^{-1} \% \overline{M}$ small.
> S3: Pick $W, \delta \in (1, \overline{M})$ meeting $\gcd(W, đ\,Đ) > 1$, $\gcd(\delta, \overline{M}) = 1$ and $\|\delta\| = đ\,Đ T$.
> S4: Compute $\alpha \leftarrow \delta^{(\bar{\sigma}^\delta + \delta\,W^{\delta-1})T}$, $\beta \leftarrow \delta^{W^\delta T}$, $\hbar \leftarrow (W\prod_{i=1}^{n} A_i)^{-\delta S}(\alpha\,\delta^{-1}) \% M$,
>   where $\bar{\sigma} \approx \overline{M}/2$ is a big prime.
> S5: Randomly produce pairwise distinct $\ell(1), \ldots, \ell(n) \in \Omega$.
> S6: Compute $C_i \leftarrow (A_i\,W^{\ell(i)})^\delta \% M$ for $i = 1, \ldots, n$.
> OUTPUT: $(\{C_i\}, \alpha, \beta)$ regarded as a public key;
> $(\{A_i\}, \{\ell(i)\}, W, \delta, Đ, đ, \hbar)$ as a private key;
> $(\bar{\sigma}, n, S, T, M)$ as being in common.

This algorithm is called by an identity key management algorithm.

3.1.2   Digital Signing Algorithm

Assume that *hash* is a one-way compression function — the Juna hash for example.

> INPUT: a private key $(\{A_i\}, \{\ell(i)\}, W, \delta, Đ, đ, \hbar)$; a file or message F.
> S1: Let $H \leftarrow hash(F)$, whose binary form is $b_1 \ldots b_n$.
> S2: Set $\underline{k} \leftarrow \delta \sum_{i=1}^{n} b_i\,\ell(i) \% \overline{M}$, $G_0 \leftarrow (\prod_{i=1}^{n} A_i^{-b_i})^\delta \% M$.
> S3: $\forall \bar{a} \in (1, \overline{M})$ making $(đ T) \nmid \bar{a}$ and $đ \nmid (WQ) \% \overline{M}$,
>   where $Q = (\bar{a}\,Đ + WH)\delta^{-1} \% \overline{M}$.
> S4: Compute $R \leftarrow (Q(\delta\,\hbar)^{-1})^{S^{-1}} G_0^{-1}$, $\bar{U} \leftarrow (RW^{\underline{k}-\delta})^\varrho \% M$,
> $\bar{g} \leftarrow \delta^{\bar{a}\,Đ} \% M$, $\xi \leftarrow \sum_{i=0}^{\bar{\sigma}-1} (\delta\,Q)^{\bar{\sigma}-1-i}(HW)^i \% \overline{M}$.
> S5: $\forall\, r \in [1, đ\,2^{16}]$ making $đ \nmid (r\,U S + \xi) \% \overline{M}$,
>   where $U = \bar{U}\bar{g}^r \% M$.
> S6: If $đ \nmid ((WQ)^{\bar{\sigma}-1} + \xi + r\,U S) \% \overline{M}$ then go to S5 else end.
> OUTPUT: (Q, U), a signature on the file F.

This algorithm is called by an identity confection algorithm.

3.1.3 Signature Authentication Algorithm

Assume that *hash* is the above one-way compression function.

INPUT: a public key ($\{C_i\}$, α, β); a file or message F; a signature (Q, U).
S1: Let $H \leftarrow hash(F)$, whose binary form is $b_1...b_n$.
S2: Compute $\bar{G}_1 \leftarrow \prod_{i=1}^{n} C_i^{b_i} \% M$.
S3: Compute $X \leftarrow (\alpha Q^{-1})^{QUT} \alpha^{Q^\delta} \% M$,
$\quad Y \leftarrow (\bar{G}_1^Q U^{-1})^{UST} \beta^{HQ^{\delta-1}+H^\delta} \% M$.
S4: If $X = Y$ then the signature is valid and F intact
$\quad$ else the signature is invalid or F modified.
OUTPUT: "yes" or "no".

This algorithm is called by an identity verification algorithm.

3.2 Juna Hash Function

Definition 7. Let $b_1...b_n \neq 0$ be a bit string. Then $\not{b}_i$ with $i \in [1, n]$ is called a bit shadow if it comes from such a rule [41]:

① $\not{b}_i = 0$ if $b_i = 0$;
② $\not{b}_i = 1 +$ the number of successive 0-bits before b_i if $b_i = 1$; or
③ $\not{b}_i = 1 +$ the number of successive 0-bits before $b_i +$ the number of successive 0-bits after the rightmost 1-bit if b_i is the leftmost 1-bit.

For example, let $b_1...b_8 = 01010100$, then $\not{b}_1...\not{b}_8 = 04020200$.

Definition 8. Let $\not{b}_1...\not{b}_n$ be the bit shadow string of $b_1...b_n \neq 0$. Then $\bar{b}_i = \not{b}_i 2^{\vartheta_i}$ with $i \in [1, n]$ is called a bit long-shadow, where $b_{i+(-1)^{\lfloor 2(i-1)/n \rfloor}(n/2)} = 0$ or 1 [41].

For example, let $b_1...b_8 = 01010100$, then $\bar{b}_1...\bar{b}_8 = 08020400$.

The Chaum-Heijst-Pfitzmann hash function, a non-iterative one based on a DLP, is appreciable [45].

The new non-iterative hash function is constituted of two algorithms which contain two main parameters m and n, where m denotes the bit-length of a modulus utilized in the new hash, n denotes the bit-length of a short message or a message digest from a classical hash function, and there are $80 \leq m \leq 232$ with $80 \leq m \leq n \leq 4096$.

Additionally, Λ and Ω are two integral sets. Their lengths are selected as $2^{10} \leq |\Lambda| \leq 2^{32}$ and $n \leq |\Omega| = \tilde{n} \leq 2^{32}$, and moreover make $2n^5 |\Omega| |\Lambda|^5 \geq 2^m$. Notice that $2^{10} \leq |\Lambda| \leq 2^{32}$ means $10 \leq \lceil \lg \not{P} \rceil \leq 32$.

For example, as $m = 80 \leq n$, there should be $|\Lambda| = 2^{10}$ and $|\Omega| = n$; as $m = 96 \leq n$, should $|\Lambda| = 2^{12}$ and $|\Omega| = n$; as $m = 112 \leq n$, should $|\Lambda| = 2^{14}$ and $|\Omega| = n$; as $m = 128 \leq n$, should $|\Lambda| = 2^{16}$ and $|\Omega| = 2^{12}$; as $m = 232 \leq n$, should $|\Lambda| = 2^{32}$ and $|\Omega| = 2^{32}$.

3.2.1 Initialization Algorithm

This algorithm is employed by an authoritative third party or the owner of a key pair, and only needs to be executed one time.

> INPUT: the bit-length m of a modulus with $80 \leq m \leq 232$;
> the item-length n of a sequence with $80 \leq m \leq n \leq 4096$;
> the maximal prime $\bar{P}$ with $10 \leq \lceil \lg \bar{P} \rceil \leq 32$;
> the size $\tilde{n}$ of the set Ω with $2\tilde{n}n^5\bar{P}^5 \geq 2^m$ and $n \leq \tilde{n} \leq 2^{32}$.
> S1: Produce $\Lambda \leftarrow \{2, 3, ..., \bar{P}\}$;
> produce a random coprime sequence $\{A_1, ..., A_n \mid A_i \in \Lambda\}$.
> S2: Find a prime M with $\lceil \lg \bar{M} \rceil = m$ such that $\bar{M}/2$ is a prime,
> or the least prime factor of $\bar{M}/2$ is bigger than $4n(2\tilde{n}+3)$.
> S3: Pick $W \in (1, \bar{M})$ making $\|W\| \geq 2^{m-\lceil \lg \bar{P} \rceil}$;
> pick $\delta \in (1, \bar{M})$ making $\gcd(\delta, \bar{M}) = 1$.
> S4: Randomly yield $\Omega \leftarrow \{+/-5, +/-7, ..., +/-(2\tilde{n}+3)\}$;
> randomly select pairwise distinct $\ell(i) \in \Omega$ for $i = 1, ..., n$.
> S5: Compute $C_i \leftarrow (A_i W^{\ell(i)})^\delta \% M$ for $i = 1, ..., n$.
> OUTPUT: an initial value $(\{C_i\}, M)$ which is public to the people.

A private parameter $(\{A_i\}, \{\ell(i)\}, W, \delta)$ may be discarded, but must not be divulged.

At S3, to seek W, let $W \equiv g^{\bar{M}/F} (\% M)$, where g is a generator of $(\mathbf{Z}_M^*, \cdot)$ obtained through Algorithm 4.80 in Sect. 4.6 of [46], and $F < 2^{\lceil \lg \bar{P} \rceil}$ is a factor of $\bar{M}$.

At S4, $\Omega = \{+/-5, +/-7, ..., +/-(2\tilde{n}+3)\}$ indicates that Ω is one of $2^{\tilde{n}}$ potential sets, indeterminate, and unknown to the public, where "$+/-$" means the selection of the "+" or "−" sign. Notice that in the arithmetic modulo $\bar{M}$, $-x$ represents $\bar{M} - x$.

3.2.2 Compression Algorithm

This algorithm is employed by one who wants to obtain a short message digest.

> INPUT: an initial value $(\{C_1, ..., C_n\}, M)$, where $\lceil \lg \bar{M} \rceil = m$ with $80 \leq m \leq n \leq 4096$;
> A short message (or a digest from a classical hash function) $b_1...b_n \neq 0$.
> S1: Set $k \leftarrow 0$, $i \leftarrow 1$.
> S2: If $b_i = 0$ then
> $\quad$ S2.1: let $k \leftarrow k+1$, $b_i \leftarrow 0$
> else
> $\quad$ S2.2: if $i = k+1$ then let $\bar{s} \leftarrow i$;
> $\quad$ S2.3: let $b_i \leftarrow k+1$, $k \leftarrow 0$.
> S3: Let $i \leftarrow i+1$;
> $\quad$ if $i \leq n$ then go to S2.
> S4: Compute $b_{\bar{s}} \leftarrow b_{\bar{s}} + k$.
> S5: Compute $\bar{d} \leftarrow \prod_{i=1}^n C_i^{\bar{b}_i} \% M$,
> $\quad$ where $\bar{b}_i = b_i 2^{\partial_i}$ with $\partial_i = b_{i+(-1)^{\lfloor 2(i-1)/n \rfloor}(n/2)}$.
> OUTPUT: a digest $\bar{d} \equiv \prod_{i=1}^n C_i^{\bar{b}_i} (\% M)$ of which the bit-length is m.

It is easily known from Definition 8 that the max of $\{b_1, \ldots, b_n\}$ is less than or equal to n when $b_1 \ldots b_n \neq 0$.

4 United Verification Platform for BFIDs and Identification Systems

4.1 Topological Structure of the Platform

The platform working in cloud computing mode and being reached through a domain name or a mobile number supplies shared storage and verification services for a wide variety of users or lessees (Fig. 7). For security, the cloudland is partitioned into an inner network and an outer network.

Between the inner network and the outer network, there is a security gateway which can prohibit illegal IP packets from invading the inner network. Additionally, the platform will have a strict identification mechanism which can prevent unauthorized

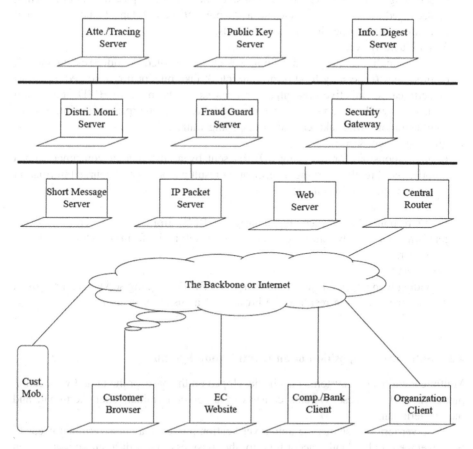

Fig. 7. Topological structure of the united verification platform for BFIDs

persons from accessing and modifying databases. The platform does not need strict encryption measures since all data on it are allowed being in a public state.

The platform is composed of a verification server, source tracing server, public key server, information digest server, distribution monitoring server, fraud guard server, short message server, IP packet server, web server, etc.

- Verification/Source Tracing Server
  Being responsible for the checking computation of BFIDs, and returning the result and relevant information to an inquirer.
- Public Key Server
  Storing all public keys of enterprises, organizations, institutions, and persons. These public keys may be accessed, but may not be modified.
- Information & Digest Server
  Storing characteristic information, description data, source information, or their digests of persons and things (commodities, bills, notes, diplomas, certificates, websites, programs, etc.).
- Distribution Monitoring Server
  Supervising and managing the warehouse-outing, delivery, passage, and marketing of packaged merchandise articles so as to prevent the overlap of sale regions and guarantee the retrospection of sale channels.
- Fraud Guard Server
  Detecting malicious programs, fishing websites, fabricated IP addresses, counterfeit commodities (especially food or drug articles), fake bills or notes, forged diplomas or certificates, imitative credentials or licenses on the basis of BFID verification results, as well as reporting occurrences to related enterprises, institutions, or administrations who take charge of disposing frauds.
- Short Message Server
  Being responsible for receiving a BFID sent by a customer or consumer with a mobile, and directly returning a verification result and a piece of source information to the customer or consumer.
- IP Packet Server
  Being responsible for receiving a program BFID from a computer outside the platform, and directly returning a verification result in the form of a IP packet to the computer.
- Web Server
  Providing web pages for question inquiry and BFID checking service, and return an answer or verification result to the browser of a customer or user.

4.2   Software Composition of an Identification System

Multiple identification systems may be developed on the basis of the united verification platform. Each of these systems consists of a server terminal, client terminal, and inquiry terminal.

A server terminal shares the united verification platform, a client terminal needs to be developed individually according to the business of a different client — an enterprise or institution for example, and an inquiry terminal also needs to be developed individually according to the medium of a different inquirer a user or customer for example.

- Software at a Server Terminal
  Including a BFID verifier, a source tracing subsystem, a distribution monitoring subsystem, a fraud guarder, a short message exchanger, an IP packet exchanger, a web page exchanger, a user register, etc.
- General Software at a Client Terminal
  Involving an asymmetric foundational operator, a one-way hash function, a key-pair generator, a key-pair keeper, a digital signer, etc.
- Individual Software at a Client Terminal
  Involving a public key cloudland storage subsystem, an identity confection subsystem, a source information transfer subsystem, a label/mark concocting subsystem, a multiple identities handling subsystem, etc.
- Software at an Inquiry Terminal
  Including identity information sensor, identity validity query subsystem, etc.

5 Applications of Idology

Obviously, idology has its applicative value in public security and network security.

5.1 Applications in Public Security

Fraud in the real world is rampant, which damages greatly the development of national economy, hence, it should be prevented at technical level.

- Banknote Anti-forgery System Based on BFIDs
  The central bank gives every banknote a BFID which is visibly printed on the surface of the banknote without a chip, and hides the private key of the central bank and the characteristic of the banknote — the currency number, par value, issuing bank name, issuing date, currency version etc. for example. The BFID sent with the mobile of a customer is checked by the united verification platform, and the platform can detect whether a BFID is imitated, and a banknote is forged through analyzing big BFID data [47].
- Diploma Anti-forgery System Based on BFIDs
  A college or university grants every graduate a diploma on which a BFID is visibly printed. The BFID conceals the private key of the college or university and the characteristic of the graduate — the name, birthday, resident ID number/social insurance number, graduating time, graduating university, specialty etc. for example. Because the ID number or social insurance number of the graduate is unique and inimitable, the BFID is also inimitable.
  When the diploma of a graduate is examined by an employer, a related BFID is sent to the united verification platform alongside of the ID card or insurance card of the graduate being examined [48].

- Food/Drug Anti-counterfeit and Source Tracing System Based on BFIDs
  A food/drug mill assigns to every food/drug article a BFID which is printed on the label of the food/drug article, covered with a layer of luminescent powder, and hides the private key of the mill and the characteristic or source information of the food/drug article — the product number, material component, production date, expiration date, mill name, mill address etc. for example.
  The coat on a BFID needs to be scraped off when it is inputted or scanned to a mobile for verification. The united verification platform will return the "True" value, source information, and marketing channel if the BFID passes the examination [26].
- Passport Anti-forgery System Oriented to Antiterrorism
  Most of terrorists utilized fake passports to sneak into intendedly attacked countries (Fig. 8) [49].

Fig. 8. Serbian magazine Blic displays a fake Syrian passport found at a scene of the Paris attacks

Therefore, to prevent passports from being forged, should let a passport contain a lightweight asymmetric identity such as a BFID and a biological characteristic. The former hides the private key of an issuing government and the personal material of a related holder, and ensures the coherence between the issuing government and the passport; the latter is the head-photo, fingerprint, or iris of the related holder which ensures the coherence between the passport and the related holder. By transmissibility, there is the coherence between the issuing government and the related holder.

The lightweight asymmetric identity should be visibly printed on a page of the passport so as to be capable of being checked in manual way through a united verification platform. Clearly, some protocols on and standards for lightweight asymmetric identities and the united verification platform should be proposed to a pertinent international association and sufficiently discussed among most nations before the final versions are concluded.

5.2   Applications in Network Security

The Internet is innately imperfect, which leaves occasions to cheaters.

- Prevention of Fictional IP Addresses
  IETF published Internet Protocol version 6 (shortly IPv6) in 1998 [50]. IPv6 adopts a 128-bit address format allowing 2128 addresses, which means that almost every device on the Internet may be assigned an IP address for identification and location definition. However, it has two prominent flaws:

① a nation identifier is not designated in the global routing prefix of an IP address;
② there is no mechanism for precluding fictional IP addresses or IP addresses fraud although there is the Internet Protocol Security (IPsec) attached to IPv6 which is developed only to prevent the content of an IP packet from being divulged as well as the source and destination addresses in an IP packet from being tampered.

Hence, IPv6+ is suggested by the authors. The dominant difference between IPv6 + and IPv6 is the partition of a source or destination address and the prevention of fictional IP addresses. In IPv6+ , the structure of a source or destination address is as follows (Fig. 9):

8 bits	24-32 bits	8-16 bits	80 bits
Nation	Domestic Routing	Subnet	Interface
ID	Indicator	ID	ID

Fig. 9. Structure of an IPv6+ address

In an IPv6+ address, the nation ID which is an 8-bit number represents the boundary of a national territory in the cyberspace, needs to be uniformly assigned among major countries, and should be coincident with the international calling code of a country — 86 being of China for example.

The domestic routing indicator which is a 24–32 bit number represents the approach to a province (state), municipality (county), city, or town.

The subnet ID which is an 8–16 bit number represents a subsystem of interconnections within a system, and it allows the components to communicate directly with each other.

The interface ID equivalent to a BFID which is an 80 bit number represents a host, router, or other device on a subnet, and hides the private key of a national cyberspace administration and the characteristic of an interface such as the domain name (globally unique), EUI-64 address (also globally unique), nation ID, domestic routing indicator, subnet ID, etc.

When a destination host receives a IP packet, it will extract a source address from the IP packet, and send the source address to the united verification platform which will check the validity of the source address with the public key of the national cyberspace administration, and return a result to the host. Note that a IP packet should be simultaneously signed with the private key of a user on a related source host.

- Dynamic Password Equivalent to a BFID
  A dynamic password of which the checking is not a direct comparison or hash comparison is confected through the optimized REESSE1+ signing scheme, hides the private key source or biologic fingerprint of a user and the characteristic of a login occasion such as the user name, login date, login time, machine name, etc., is thoroughly different on every login, and is checked with the user's public key that is fetched to a server terminal in advance. Obviously, a dynamic password is substantially equivalent to a BFID which is so short as to be capable of being checked fast.

The advantage over a classical password of a dynamic password is that it may protect a confidential fingerprint or private key source against being exposed to an eavesdropper in a transmission process or to an inside job worker at a server terminal.

- Official Document against Forgery and Tampering
  When an official document of an organization or administration is promulgated on the Internet, it should bear a BFID which is so short as to be capable of being placed at the document's file name position [35, 41]. The BFID conceals the private key of the organization or administration and the characteristic of the document — the title, script number, key words, promulgator name, promulgating date, etc. for example, is checked by the united verification platform, and can defend the document against being forged or tampered.
- Prevent Computer Viruses
  A program is given an asymmetric identity BFID by its developer, and the BFID is put in the program's file name [35, 41]. When the program is executed, the BFID will be captured, sent to the united verification platform, and verified with the public key of the developer. If the BFID is ineligible, the execution of the program will be terminated. It is impossible that a computer virus acquire an eligible BFID, and this way, computer viruses may be prevented.
- Attestation by a Real Name against Privacy Divulgence in Cyberspace
  When a citizen registers at a server with his own real identity, he needs to input from a keyboard his account-name, BFID (equivalent to a real name), profession, affiliation, etc., where the BFID will be sent to the united verification platform storing a variety of public keys for examination. Note that a traditional password is not necessary for registration due to a dynamic password being available.

Such a BFID as a network identity of a citizen hides the private key of a national population administration and the characteristic of a resident such as the legal identity — the Chinese ID number for example, legal name, gender, home address, telephone number etc. Note that the Chinese ID number despite being nationally unique is not allowed to be inputted into a server on the registration of a citizen because it contains the privacy birth date of the citizen.

6   Conclusion

Omnipresent fraud in both the real world and the cyberspace causes the international society giant economic losses [1–4]. The prevention of fraud needs not only behavioral legislation but also technical innovation. The latter is more urgent.

The logic makes it clear that the prevention of fraud is essentially the identification of a person or thing in the real world and the cyberspace.

Facts elucidate that ubiquitous old-line symmetric identities are incompetent for anti-fraud, and asymmetric identities represent a new direction in anti-fraud.

Extensive and favorable application demands leads the naissance of a new discipline — idology which is the study of knowledge on identifications of persons or things in brief.

The aim of idology is the prevention of fraud while the aim of cryptology is the prevention of secret-outing, and thus idology should be independently considered and treated. If they are confused, then the fulfillment of anti-fraud tasks all over the world will be affected severely.

Along with the coming of quantum computer era, researches on post-quantum idology which is resistant to quantum computation attack namely Shor algorithm attack will be made [51].

Many problems relevant to idology are faced with us, and need to be seriously resolved.

Acknowledgment.   The authors would like to thank the Acad. Jiren Cai, Acad. Zhongyi Zhou, Acad. Changxiang Shen, Acad. Zhengyao Wei, Acad. Binxing Fang, Acad. Guangnan Ni, Acad. Andrew C. Yao, Acad. Jinpeng Huai, Acad. Wen Gao, Prof. Jie Wang, Rese. Hanliang Xu, Rese. Dengguo Feng, Rese. Dali Liu, Rese. Qiquan Guo, Rese. Rui Yu, Prof. Zhiying Wang, Prof. Ron Rivest, Prof. Moti Yung, Prof. Dingzhu Du, Acad. Xiangke Liao, Acad. Wenhua Ding, Prof. Huaimin Wang, Prof. Jianfeng Ma, Prof. Heyan Huang, Prof. Zhong Chen, Prof. Jiwu Jing, Prof. Gongxuan Zhang, Prof. Yixian Yang, Prof. Maozhi Xu, Prof. Bing Chen, Prof. Xuejia Lai, Prof. Yongfei Han, Prof. Yupu Hu, Prof. Ping Luo, Acad. Wei Li, Acad. Xicheng Lu, Prof. Dingyi Pei, Prof. Huanguo Zhang, Prof. Mulan Liu, Prof. Bogang Lin, Prof. Renji Tao, Prof. Quanyuan Wu, and Prof. Zhichang Qi for their important suggestions, corrections, and helps.

References

1. Schuman, M.: Why Alibaba's Massive Counterfeit Problem Will Never be Solved. Forbes, 23 November 2015
2. Levy, A.: Amazon's Chinese Counterfeit Problem is Getting Worse. CNBC, 8 July 2016
3. Walsh, D.: Fake Diplomas, Real Cash: Pakistani Company Axact Reaps Millions. The New York Times, 17 May 2015

4. Vedelago, C., Houston, C.: Australia Flooded with Fake $50 Notes So Good They Fool Banks. Sydney Morning Herald, 28 February 2016

5. Mäntysaari, P.: The Law of Corporate Finance: General Principles and EU Law. Volume III: Funding, Exit, Takeovers. Springer, Heidelberg (2010)

6. Horowitz, M.: Router security - subnets and IP addresses, 3 June 2015. http://routersecurity. org/ipaddresses.php

7. Stallings, W.: Cryptography and Network Security: Principles and Practice, 5th edn. Prentice-Hall, New Jersey (2010)

8. McDowell, M.: Avoiding social engineering and phishing attacks. US Computer Emergency Readiness Team, 22 October 2009. https://www.us-cert.gov/ncas/tips/ST04–014. Accessed 06 Feb 2013

9. Bicknell, D.E., Laporte, G.M.: Forged and counterfeit documents. In: Wiley Encyclopedia of Forensic Science. Wiley, September 2009

10. Lichter, S.: Federal and state wiretap act regulation of keyloggers in the workplace. Harvard J. Law Technol. (2012)

11. Editors of the American Heritage Dictionaries: American Heritage Dictionary of the English Language, 5th edn. Houghton Mifflin Harcourt Publishing, November 2011

12. Editors of the American Heritage Dictionaries: American Heritage Roget's Thesaurus. Houghton Mifflin Harcourt Publishing, July 2013

13. Yu, H., Li, N.: The Around Five Millenniums of China (in Chinese). Huawen Press, Beijing (2009)

14. Oracle: Attestation of Identity Information, May 2006. http://www.economist.com

15. Paton, W.R. (Translator): Polybius: The Histories, vol. III, Books 5–8 (Loeb Classical Library No. 138). Harvard University Press, January 1923

16. Ran, Q.: The Chinese History Illustrated by Pictures (in Chinese). Higher Education Press, Beijing (2011)

17. Meggs, P.B.: A History of Graphic Design, 3rd edn. Wiley, New York (1998)

18. Richardson, G.: Brand names before the industrial revolution (NBER Working Paper No. 13930). National Bureau of Economic Research, April 2008

19. McGrew, S.P.: Holographic Technology for Anti-counterfeit Security: Present and Future. Holo-pack & Holo-print Asia, Singapore (1996)

20. Yang, C.: Investigation into the shady deal in anti-counterfeit industry (in Chinese). Bus. Circles 4, 48–50 (2002)

21. Denso Adc: QR Code Essentials, 31 March 2011. www.denso-adc.com/pdf/qrcode

22. Jain, A., Hong, L., Pankanti, S.: Biometric identification. Commun. ACM **43**(2), 91–98 (2000)

23. Olsen, R.D.: The chemical composition of palmar sweat. Fingerprint Ident. Mag. **53**(10), 3–7, 14–16, 23 (1972)

24. Hueske, E.: Firearms and Fingerprints (Essentials of Forensic Science Set, 7-Volumes). Infobase Publishing, New York (2008)

25. Schneier, B.: Fake anti-counterfeiting holograms, 13 February 2007. https://www.schneier. com/blog/archives/2007/02/fake_anticounte.html

26. Su, S., Li, N., Lü, S.: Drug anti-forgery and tracing system based on lightweight asymmetric identities. In: Chau, M., Wang, G.Alan, Chen, H. (eds.) PAISI 2015. LNCS, vol. 9074, pp. 82–90. Springer, Cham (2015). doi:10.1007/978-3-319-18455-5_6

27. Walton, C.A.: Portable radio frequency emitting identifier. U.S. Patent 4384288, 17 May 1983

28. Sarma, S.E., Weis, S.A., Engels, D.W.: RFID systems and security and privacy implications. In: Kaliski, B.S., Koç, ç, Paar, C. (eds.) CHES 2002. LNCS, vol. 2523, pp. 454–469. Springer, Heidelberg (2003). doi:10.1007/3-540-36400-5_33

29. Stajano, F.: Security in pervasive computing. In: Hutter, D., Müller, G., Stephan, W., Ullmann, M. (eds.) Security in Pervasive Computing. LNCS, vol. 2802, pp. 6–8. Springer, Heidelberg (2004). doi:10.1007/978-3-540-39881-3_3

30. Hu, X.: An innovation the same sharp as a sword is created through the ten years (in Chinese). Inf. Securi. Commun. Priv. 6, 27–29 (2012)

31. Zou, W., Liu, S.: A Staffer of CSRC Who Was Involved the Inside Dealing and the Forging of Official Documents and Stamps Is Required to Aid in the Investigation (in Chinese). Beijing Youth Daily, 26 August 2015

32. ElGamal, T.: A public-key cryptosystem and a signature scheme based on discrete logarithms. IEEE Trans. Inf. Theory 31(4), 469–472 (1985)

33. Blake, I.F., Seroussi, G., Smart, N.P.: Elliptic Curves in Cryptography. Cambridge University Press, Cambridge, UK (1999)

34. Rivest, R.L., Shamir, A., Adleman, L.M.: A method for obtaining digital signatures and public-key cryptosystems. Commun. ACM 21(2), 120–126 (1978)

35. Su, S., Lü, S.: A public key cryptosystem based on three new provable problems. Theor. Comput. Sci. 426–427, 91–117 (2012)

36. Su, S., Lü, S., Fan, X.: Asymptotic granularity reduction and its application. Theor. Comput. Sci. 412(39), 5374–5386 (2011)

37. Davis, M.: The Undecidable: Basic Papers on Undecidable Propositions, Unsolvable Problems and Computable Functions. Dover Publications, Mineola (2004)

38. Sipser, M.: Introduction to the Theory of Computation. PWS Publishing, Boston (1997)

39. Menezes, A.: Elliptic Curve Public Key Cryptosystems. Kluwer Academic Publishers, Boston (1993)

40. Schneier, B.: Applied Cryptography: Protocols, Algorithms, and Source Code in C, 2nd edn. Wiley, New York (1996)

41. Su, S., Xie, T., Lü, S.: A provably secure non-iterative hash function resisting birthday attack. Theor. Comput. Sci. 654, 128–142 (2016)

42. Su, S., Lü, S.: REESSE1+ • Reward • Proof by experiment • A new approach to proof of P ! = NP. Cornell University Library (2009). http://arxiv.org/pdf/0908.0482. Accessed 2014

43. Yang, A.: Math 25: introduction to number theory (Class 20 Notes). Department of Mathematics, Dartmouth College, November 2011. http://www.math.dartmouth.edu/~m25f11/notes/class20.pdf

44. Cohen, H.: A Course in Computational Algebraic Number Theory. Springer (2000)

45. Chaum, D., Heijst, E., Pfitzmann, B.: Cryptographically Strong Undeniable Signatures, Unconditionally Secure for the Signer. In: Feigenbaum, J. (ed.) CRYPTO 1991. LNCS, vol. 576, pp. 470–484. Springer, Heidelberg (1992). doi:10.1007/3-540-46766-1_38

46. Menezes, A., Oorschot, P.V., Vanstone, S.: Handbook of Applied Cryptography. CRC Press, London, UK (2001)

47. Su, S., Cai, Y., Shen, C.: The banknote anti-forgery system based on digital signature algorithms. In: Yang, C.C., et al. (eds.) ISI 2008. LNCS, vol. 5075, pp. 44–49. Springer, Heidelberg (2008). doi:10.1007/978-3-540-69304-8_5

48. Dai, Y., Su, S.: A diploma anti-forgery system based on lightweight digital signatures. In: CIS2014, IEEE, November 2014

49. Izadi, E.: (Under Paris Terror Attack) There's a Booming Black Market for Fake Syrian Passports. Washington Post, 21 November 2015

50. Deering, S., Hinden, R.: Internet Protocol Version 6 (IPv6) Specification (RFC 2460). The Internet Society, December 1998

51. Shor, P.W.: Polynomial-time algorithms for prime factorization and discrete logarithms on a quantum computer. SIAM J. Comput. 26(5), 1484–1509 (1997)

Author Index

Printed in the United States
By Bookmasters

Printed in the United States
By Bookmasters